Webb Society Deep-Sky Observer's Handbook
Volume 3: Open and Globular Clusters

Webb Society Deep–Sky Observer's Handbook

Volume 3
Open and Globular Clusters

Compiled by the Webb Society
Editor: Kenneth Glyn Jones, F.R.A.S.
Written and Illustrated by Edmund S. Barker, F.R.A.S.

With a foreword by Professor Helen Sawyer Hogg
(David Dunlap Observatory, University of Toronto)

Enslow Publishers
Hillside, New Jersey 07205

1980

Library of Congress Cataloging in Publication Data

Webb Society.
    Webb Society deep-sky observer's handbook.

    First published in 1975– under title: The Webb
Society observers handbook.
    Includes bibliographies.
    CONTENTS: v. 1. Double Stars.– v. 2. Planetary and
gaseous nebulae.– v. 3. Open and Globular Clusters.
    1. Astronomy–Observers' manuals. I. Jones, Kenneth
Glyn. II. Title.

QB64.W35 1979   523   78-31260
In the U.S.A.: ISBN 0-89490-034-X (vol.3)
In the U.K.: ISBN 07188 2468 7 (vol.3)

Manufactured in the United States of America
10 9 8 7 6 5 4 3

To Professor Helen Sawyer Hogg,
Pre-eminent observer of Star Clusters,
With gratitude and affection

CONTENTS

LIST OF ILLUSTRATIONS

Field drawings of 176 Open Clusters will be found
between pages 48 and 135, and a further sample of
6 Open Clusters on pages 198 and 199.

Field Drawings of 53 Globular Clusters will be
found between pages 156 and 183.

FOREWORD

Some watchers of the sky regard star clusters as the most beautiful objects in the heavens. Several millenia ago the open cluster, the Pleiades, so caught the imagination of some early peoples that they regulated their year by its heliacal rising. Tennyson captured their beauty when he wrote that the Pleiades stars "Glitter like a swarm of fireflies tangled in a silver braid". Eye-catching young and profligate blue-white stars are a feature of many open clusters, some of which have red stars too.

Only after the development of telescopes did globular clusters come to be noticed with their hundreds of pinpoints of light. Their importance was recognized as early as 1714 when Halley shrewdly suggested that the luminous spots, including the globular cluster later numbered 13 by Messier, "cannot fail to occupy Spaces immensely great". Though globular clusters are the oldest objects in the sky, they are by no means static, as Auwers, Luther and Pogson learned in 1860 when they saw Messier 80 in Scorpius change its appearance with a seventh magnitude nova in its core. When and where will the next such nova be seen in a globular cluster? Frequently change can be noticed in the clusters numbered 2, 3 and 5 by Messier when one of their brightest stars brightens and fades as a periodic variable.

It is small wonder that sky watchers with telescopes, or even just binoculars, are eager to observe star clusters. This volume is a convenient pathway and guide to such observations. For a century great encouragement has been given to sky observers, first by the Rev. T.W. Webb and later by the Society founded in his honour. My sincere congratulations go to the Webb Society and its editor Kenneth Glyn Jones for producing this Handbook on Star Clusters as Volume 3 of the Webb Society Deep-Sky Observer's Handbook.

Helen Sawyer Hogg

General Preface

Named after the Rev. T.W. Webb (1807-1885), an eminent amateur astronomer and author of the classic <u>Celestial Objects for Common Telescopes</u>, the Webb Society exists to encourage the study of double stars and deep-sky objects. It has members in almost every country where amateur astronomy flourishes. It has a number of sections, each under a director with wide experience in the particular field, the main ones being double stars, nebulae and clusters, minor planets, supernova watch and astrophotography. Publications include a Quarterly Journal containing articles and special features, book reviews and section reports that cover the society's activities. Membership is open to anyone whose interests are compatible. Application forms and answers to queries are available from Dr. G.S. Whiston, Secretary, Webb Society, "Chestnuts", 1 Cramhurst Lane, Witley, Surrey, England.

Webb's <u>Celestial Objects for Common Telescopes</u>, first published in 1859, must have been among the most popular books of its kind ever written. Running through six editions by 1917, it still is in print although the text is of more historical than practical interest to the amateur of today. Not only has knowledge of the universe been transformed totally by modern developments, but the present generation of amateur astronomers has telescopes and other equipment that even the professional of Webb's day would have envied.

The aim of the new <u>Webb Society Deep-Sky Observer's Handbook</u> is to provide a series of observer's manuals that do justice to the equipment that is available today and to cover fields that have not been adequately covered by other organisations of amateurs. We have endeavoured to make these guides the best of their kind: they are written by experts, some of them professional astronomers, who have had considerable practical experience with the problems and pleasures of the amateur astronomer. The manuals can be used profitably by the beginner, who will find much to stimulate his enthusiasm and imagination. However, they are designed primarily for the more experienced amateur who seeks greater scope for the the exercise of his skills.

Each handbook is complete with respect to its subject. The reader is given an adequate historical and theoretical basis for a modern understanding of the physical role of the objects covered in the wider context of the universe. He is provided with a thorough exposition of observing methods, including the construction and operation of ancillary equipment such as micrometers and simple spectroscopes. Each volume contains a detailed and comprehensive catalogue of objects for the amateur to locate and to observe with an eye made more perceptive by the knowledge he has gained.

We hope that these volumes will enable the reader to extend his abilities, to exploit his telescope to its limit, and to tackle the challenging difficulties of new fields of observation with confidence of success.

Preface
Volume 3: Open and Globular Clusters

The two kinds of celestial objects covered in this volume can both be loosely described as star-clusters. However, in astronomical terms they differ in almost all respects. Open clusters are young in the evolutionary scale and most of them are comparatively near to us in our Galaxy: the globular clusters on the other hand have histories that go back to the very beginnings of galaxy-formation, and some of them are so distant that they may be virtually free of the gravitational field of the Galaxy.

For the amateur observer they present not only very different visual aspects, but also require very different methods of observation. The open clusters may often be difficult to separate from the background star-field, but they are generally easy to resolve: in drawing at the telescope, however, great skill and patience are required to produce an accurate representation. Globular clusters are usually conspicuous in appearance, but for a large number of them, the resolution into constituent stars may tax the observer's visual acuity to the utmost.

The imagination may well be stirred by the sight of one of the 'great' globular clusters - such as omega Centauri or M13 - in all the glory of its myriad stars: the open clusters have a more aesthetic appeal, and not even the finest astronomical photograph can do justice to the prismatic beauty of the double-cluster in Perseus (h and chi Persei) or the 'Jewel Box' in Crux as seen in even the most modest of amateur telescopes.

This volume provides a more than adequate historical and theoretical background for the reader to appreciate the importance of both classes of star-clusters in their different astronomical aspects. Expert guidance is given in the selection, location and classification of objects in each field, and as in earlier volumes, useful hints are provided on observing technique and recording. In addition a selected catalogue in each class, complete with numerous field drawings, has been compiled from observations made by members of the Webb Society over the years. Observers will find this an invaluable aid to recognition for many of the more 'difficult' objects, and a useful comparison for their own observations. Altogether, some 205 open clusters (176 of them with drawings) and 63 globular clusters (53 with drawings) are included.

Almost the whole of the text has been written in this instance by Edmund Barker, who as Director of the Nebulae and Clusters Section, has co-ordinated the many deep-sky observing schemes undertaken world-wide by members of the Webb Society. In addition, Ed Barker's skill as a draughtsman is manifest throughout the whole of this volume: we are indeed fortunate that such talents are given so unstintingly.

As with all our productions, the Editor wishes to acknowledge with gratitude the contribution of our Publications Officer, Eddie Moore, who has kept a watchful and expert eye on all stages of preparation of this volume.

We extend our thanks also to Ridley M. Enslow Jr., President of Enslow Publishers, for his enthusiastic support in our publishing activities, and especially for his guidance and expertise in the reproduction of the all-important field drawings in this and previous volumes.

Finally, we wish to express to Professor Helen Sawyer Hogg our deep gratitude for doing us the signal honour of accepting the dedication of this volume, and for so generously contributing a foreward. Her eminence in astronomy, especially in the field of globular cluster observation and analytical research, is internationall acknowledged, as is her abiding interest in and encouragement of many o the activities of amateur astronomers.

GENERAL INTRODUCTION.

The degree to which the maximum amount of information can be obtained from any object under study is a direct consequence of the materials and method used, and nowhere is this more so than in the field of observational astronomy. Often, however, the method can be seen to be in advance of the means, and the time comes when abilities in visual observation have virtually exhausted the potential of a given telescope. It is at this point that financial questions arise; greater light-gathering qualities demand a larger aperture, and this in turn requires a considerable cash outlay. The differences between telescopes of, for example, 8 and 16-inches aperture are sizeable, both from the point of view of performance and of cost. If we take galaxies as a class of object for visual observation, no one who has access to a 16-inch would willingly return to the use of an 8-inch. Bearing this in mind, it is therefore worthwhile realizing that deep-sky objects do exist in which a high percentage of information can be obtained with the use of relatively inexpensive instrumentation, and most of the present volume is concerned with such objects.

In the field of visual observation of star clusters, the observer is confronted with objects that, in a large number of cases, exhibit a considerable amount of detail. Even quite small telescopes are capable of fully resolving numbers of open clusters, while many globular clusters will allow at least peripheral resolution to be obtained, and in a number of cases total resolution is the order. With such morphology being relatively easy to determine, star clusters may legitimately be said to outrank other deep-sky objects in the context of resolution of constituent parts.

Unlike many nebulae and galaxies, open and globular clusters are (with inevitable exceptions) not objects that present extreme problems in locating. Indeed, many examples abound where visual observation will reveal an object that can well-nigh dominate its particular field, whereas a photograph of the region with a large telescope increases field star distribution to such an extent that the cluster merges to a large degree with the field.

Over the whole sky a large number of clusters is shown on the Atlas Coeli charts, and a selection of objects not plotted in Coeli is one of the aims of the present volume. A number of such clusters have been observed, and appear in the catalogue sections while a selection of others will be found in the list of additional objects. We have endeavoured to achieve an adequate balance between the more well-known objects that many observers are aquainted with, and lesser-known but often equally interesting clusters.

Observers invariably find themselves gravitating towards a particular type of object upon which they spend the greater part of their observing time. This is illustrated in this volume, where the open clusters are primarily the province of a few observers who have concentrated to a large degree upon these objects. Interest and

General Introduction.

determination can produce qualitative and comprehensive results
in observational astronomy, and hopefully the results set out in
the present catalogues will act as a catalyst for those not yet
aware of the variety of objects within a single class, as well
as showing how much can be achieved with moderate telescopes.

Acknowledgements.

David Allen contributed to the Appendix on cluster distances
as well as contributing many observations to the catalogues.
David Pike and John Alexander of the Royal Greenwich Observatory
kindly supplied data on globular clusters and stellar associations,
while further data on open clusters was supplied by Guy Hurst.
Much of the research for this volume was undertaken at the library
of the Royal Astronomical Society and at University College London.
The writer expresses his thanks to the Leverhulme Research Awards
Committee for a research grant to aid in the compilation of this
Handbook.

PART ONE : OPEN CLUSTERS.

HISTORICAL REVIEW.

That some stars are associated in cluster-like forms was noted by the earliest astronomers: the Hyades and Pleiades (both true clusters) for example, have always been recognised as distinct asterisms within the larger grouping of the constellation Taurus. Clusters smaller than the Pleiades, however, defied resolution by optically unaided eyesight, and the few that were observed before the invention of the telescope were all classed under the vague description of 'nebulae' (little clouds) or 'nebulosae' (cloudy (stars)). Ptolemy listed seven of these, but only four, the double cluster in Perseus (h and χ Persei), Praesepe in Cancer, M7 in Scorpio and the 'cloudy convolutions' of Coma Berenices are true clusters, the other three being small asterisms.

The Persian astronomer, Al Sufi, who, in about AD 954, was the first to report the existence of the Andromeda Nebula, also listed the 'nebulae' of Ptolemy and added the little asterism which includes 4 and 5 Vulpeculae, and which has become well-known as 'Briochi's' cluster. He also included the star cluster around omicron Velorum (IC 2391). Other false clusters of various kinds were added in the star catalogues of Ulugh Begh and Tycho Brahe, but with the advent of the telescope in the hands of Galileo, we first arrive at the recognition that 'the nebula called Praesepe is not one star only but a mass of more than forty small stars'. Galileo thought that _all_ nebulae could be resolved into component stars, and this impression was to persist for several centuries.

As telescopes improved in light-grasp and resolution, many new and diverse nebulous objects were discovered, including the open clusters M8 (Flamsteed in 1680), M11 (Kirch, 1681), NGC 2244 and M41 (Flamsteed, 1690 and 1702), M50 (Cassini, 1711). In the years 1745-46 the French astronomer de Chésaux discovered M6, IC 4665, NGC 6633, M16, M25, M35, and made a more-or-less successful attempt to differentiate between nebulae which were composed of stars and those 'rightly-styled nebulae which when seen in the largest telescopes, never appear as anything but white clouds.

Two of the well-known open clusters in Auriga, M36 and M38, were discovered and demonstrated to consist only of stars by Le Gentil in 1749, (M37 was found by Messier in 1764). In 1751-52 the Abbe Lacaille, in his expedition to the Cape of Good Hope, compiled a list of 42 nebulous objects of the southern skies, which included some 16 new, genuine open clusters. Lacaille also attempted a more rigorous classification of the 'nebulae' he had found, dividing them into Class I - nebulae without stars; Class II - nebulous stars in clusters and Class III - stars accompanied by nebulosity. This scheme did in fact give a rough separation of globular clusters, open clusters and diffuse nebulae, but the distinction was not entirely sharp nor consistent enough to be meaningful at the time.

Neither Charles Messier, nor his imitator in the compilation of catalogues of nebulae, J.E. Bode, made any attempt to classify the nebulae they listed, but the former gathered in his fruitful net a dozen new open clusters, although one of the finest of these, M67 in Cancer, was first discovered by J.G. Koehler at Dresden in 1778.

It was, of course, Wm. Herschel who made the great leap forward both in the discovery of new nebulae and in a more rigorous classification of them. His eight categories, from I (bright nebulae) to VIII (coarsely scattered clusters) begin to show divisions which are meaningful, and although he did not include a separate class for globular clusters, he used the term as a description of many objects we now know to be of that class. The open or galactic clusters, as might be expected, are found among those objects he classified in the categories VI (very compressed and rich clusters) VII (compressed clusters of small and large stars) and VIII (coarsely scattered clusters).

However, even Herschel's catalogues, and their successor, the NGC, did not always succeed in giving a clear separation between open and globular clusters. Even now, we know several objects – such as the well-known M71 in Sagitta – so indeterminate in form that the distinction is difficult to apply, at least purely on morphological grounds.

It was the recognition by Walter Baade in 1944 of the existence of two separate populations of stars in our Galaxy (the young Population I stars of the disc and the older Population II stars of the halo) which served to distinguish more clearly the differences between the open and globular clusters.

1. O-ASSOCIATIONS.

It would be inappropriate to commence a survey of the various factors pertaining to open clusters without first considering those stellar groups known as O-associations and their relation to open clusters. These two types of star groups are similar in many ways, and in some cases are found to be closely linked.

To define a true distinction between O-associations and open clusters is not easy: if we must pinpoint a difference it would have to be that of linear diameter, which, for the associations, is typically of the order of 100 pc. The lower limit of linear size for O-associations would seem to be about 30 pc, and we can compare this with the lower limit for open clusters, which hovers around a figure of 1 pc. The diameters of associations are, however, quite difficult to determine; membership and hence intrinsic size for any stellar group posing many problems, and thus the membership aspect of O-associations can be seen to parallel that of open clusters. Even for the smaller associations recognition of all member stars is difficult, but at least in such cases the boundaries are fairly well-defined, while with increasing size they become considerably more vague.

As is the case with open clusters, O-associations are unstable groups, and under the relentless shearing effects of galactic rotation they will eventually disperse into the surrounding star fields. Many associations show an extreme overall ellipticity while others display no tendency towards elongation in the galactic plane, and this furnishes us with a clue regarding the ages of associations. Those stars in an association which are closer to the galactic centre move at a greater speed than those which are more distant, and as a consequence of this an association will gradually spread out around the centre of the Galaxy. Theory shows that, by this action, an association will undergo a doubling of its length on a time scale of about 30×10^6 yr. For associations younger than this, their respective expansion velocities will mask the elongation process. At the upper end of the age scale, where we are concerned with times over twice that of the above, the process of dissolution will be well advanced. The Sco-Cen association, for example, displays a quite pronounced elongation which is indicative of an age of 70×10^6 yr. In contrast, the association around zeta Per, covering an area of 6° in the sky, is a much younger group, with an age of only about 10^6 yr.

The Sco-Cen association contains the well-known dark clouds near rho Oph, and also contains a number of sub-groups. Other associations also harbour the latter, e.g. Cep OB2, where the open clusters Tr 37 and NGC 7160 reside. Connections between clusters and associations are quite common, and in the present catalogue clusters linked with

O-Associations.

O-associations will be referred to in the data sections preceding
the visual observations.

Finally we must consider the question of initial identification
of an O-association. This is made by determining a region where
the density of stars of types O-B2 shows a larger-than-mean field
density than is acceptable as a chance arrangement. Where this is
the case, further work is necessary in order to obtain data on
membership. An O-association will give a fairly well-defined
colour-magnitude diagram as long as its back-to-front ratio is not
too great (for full details of colour-magnitude diagrams see
Chapter 2). Distances to associations can be estimated from the
proper motions of the constituent stars, the distance of the
Sco-Cen association being about 170 pc. In Figure 1 below is shown,
projected on to the galactic plane, O-B2 associations within a
distance of 1000 pc of the Sun.

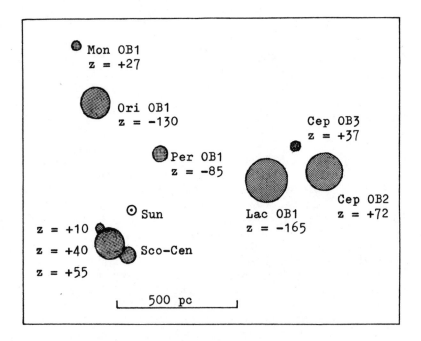

Figure 1. Positions of O-B2 associations within 1000 pc of the Sun.
z = distances in pc above (+) and
below (-) the galactic plane.

2. GALACTIC OPEN CLUSTERS.

INTRODUCTION.

Studies of star clusters have a twofold purpose, namely to obtain as fully as possible an understanding of their evolution, both past and future, and to relate this to the overall structure and evolution of the Galaxy. Both observational and theoretical data is required in this context, and in this chapter we shall briefly consider the various aspects of this work in the field of open clusters.

The chapter is divided into five sections: 1. Classification; 2. Relation to the Galaxy; 3. Cluster morphology; 4. Stellar populations and 5. Colour-Magnitude diagrams. These sections give information on cluster lifetimes as a function of stellar motions and galactic rotation, age derivations, the relation of clusters to the spiral structure of the Galaxy, individual cluster stars and, finally, cluster reddening. The latter has a bearing upon the important question of distance derivation, which will be considered for both open and globular clusters in Appendix 3.

1. Classification.

The classification of open clusters with which the majority of amateurs will be familiar is that of Shapley, who devised the following scheme: (c) very loose and irregular; (d) loose and poor; (e) intermediate rich; (f) fairly rich; (g) considerably rich and concentrated. This gives a good outline of basic cluster morphology, but is now superseded by a classification scheme which originated with Trumpler and which, besides giving a brief description of cluster structure, also furnishes details on stellar membership. Details of this classification are shown below.

I   Detached with strong central concentration.
II   Detached with little central concentration.
III   Detached with no central concentration.
IV   Not well detached but apparently like a
      strong field concentration.

These Roman numerals are followed by Arabic numerals, which are used to convey information on the luminosity function of the brightest stars (for details on luminosity functions see section 3). Finally, letters are used to denote the number of stars.

p   poor, less than 50 stars.
m   medium rich, 50 - 100 stars.
r   rich, over 100 stars.

Thus, to take the cluster NGC 6871 as an example, the Trumpler classification is IV 3 p. This particular scheme is used in the catalogue of open clusters to be found in Part Three of this Handbook. In section 3 we shall consider the morphology of open clusters further, and in particular its relation to field star distribution and the question of cluster recognition.

Galactic Open Clusters.

2. Relation to the Galaxy.

Open clusters are to be found inhabiting two population groups in the Galaxy; young clusters, along with O and B stars, occur in the extreme Population I regions, older clusters in intermediate Population I. Stellar populations will be discussed in section 4, and we shall therefore, in this section, consider the role of open clusters in defining spiral structure and also the association of clusters and nebulosity.

The spatial distribution of open clusters varies as a function of galactic latitude, and this can only be ascertained by obtaining distance determinations that are as accurate as possible. Once the cluster distances have been derived, then it is possible to arrive at figures showing their distances perpendicular to the galactic plane. These, as we have seen in Figure 1, with regard to stellar associations, are defined by the letter z, which denotes these distances in pc. In star atlases, such as Atlas Coeli, the majority of open clusters appear within the confines of the Milky Way iso-photes. This, however, gives us no indication of their distribution in z, nor does it show how clusters can aid in defining the spiral structure of the Galaxy, as the great circle of the Milky Way, seen with the eye, is comprised of different spiral arms. In some cases, e.g., Cygnus, we are looking along a spiral arm, while in others, e.g., Auriga, our viewpoint is essentially at right angles.

Nearby clusters such as the Hyades and Pleiades appear to the eye as being outside the apparent boundaries of the galactic plane. This is purely a result of their small distances from the solar system, and the further we see the more clusters will appear to be located within the Milky Way confines. Nevertheless, the Hyades are at a fair distance from the galactic plane, with z = -23, while another naked-eye cluster, Mel 111, better known, perhaps, as the Coma star cluster, has z = +85.

As we approach the plane of the galaxy the space density of open clusters increases, and this is a suitable point to discuss clusters as delineators of spiral structure.

In Figure 2 overleaf the distribution of 81 clusters is shown projected on to the galactic plane. The circle enclosing a dot defining the position of the sun. The delineation of sections of three spiral arms is easily apparent, the section at the upper right being the Perseus arm, the central section, including the sun, the Carina - Cygnus arm and the lower section the Sagittarius arm. A further correlation can be made by plotting H II regions, H I regions and stellar associations on to such a diagram. These too will be found to be indicators of spiral structure, and occupy similar positions to those of the open clusters.

Galactic Open Clusters.

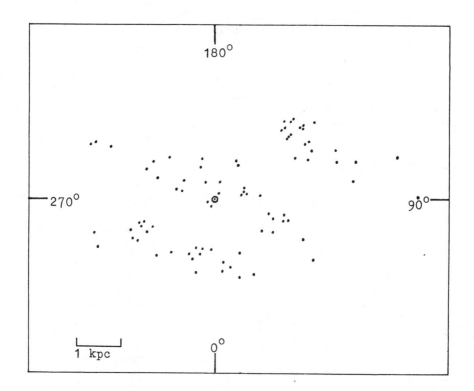

Figure 2. Distribution on the galactic
plane of 81 open clusters, showing the
delineation of three spiral arms.

On the preceding page we have mentioned how H II regions can be
fitted to the cluster plotting shown in Figure 2. It will thus be
obvious that in many cases associations of clusters and nebulosity
occur, and we shall briefly discuss such amalgams below.

Obvious associations of nebulosity and clusters are objects
such as M8 (comprising the cluster NGC 6530 and the bright and
dark nebulosity catalogued as NGC 6523) and M16. A further example
is M42, although here the cluster aspect is not as obvious as in
previous two cases.

An important effect of dark nebulosity is its ability to dim
starlight, and clusters associated with nebulosity will often be
quite heavily reddened by obscuring material. This dark nebulosity
is apparent enough when seen in conjunction with regions of bright
nebulae, as is the case with M8, but often no bright matter is
seen, and in such cases where a cluster is affected by interstellar
material, photometry can supply details of the dimming. The young

Galactic Open Clusters.

cluster IC 348 lies within a region of dark material which contains at least one heavily obscured luminous star, and it is therefore highly likely that the visible part of IC 348 is only a small part of the total.

Bearing in mind the patchy nature of the interstellar medium, it is evident that the effects of this upon clusters will vary quite considerably. Absorption figures range from as low as 0.15 mag for NGC 6281 to over 12 mag for a recently discovered cluster. Further details of clusters and nebulosity will be found in Chapter 4, while below, in Table 1, we show the diameters, in pc, of selected associations of clusters and nebulosity.

Table 1. Clusters and Associated Nebulosity.

Association.	Diam. C.(pc)	Diam. Neb.(pc)
NGC 1893/IC 410	18	25
2175	8	15
2244	12	50
2264	7	7
2579	4	150
6514 (M20)	14	14
6523/30 (M8)	21	40
6611 (M16)	6	30
IC 1805	12	90
1848	14	30
Cr 69	8	8
302	35	30

3. Cluster Morphology.

In this section we shall concentrate primarily upon the problems that can be encountered in identifying open clusters. It may seem at first thought that nothing could be simpler than defining any open cluster; that any not-too-compressed, globular-like object could be nothing but an open cluster, and vice versa. This, however, is not the case, for it must be realised that morphology alone is not the determining factor in cluster recognition. Many other factors are valid, not the least being the types of stars comprising any cluster, be it open or globular.

In the past, difficulties have often been encountered in the field of cluster classification, it being uncertain whether to assign some clusters to either the open or globular category. Examples of certain individual cases will be given in Chapter 7, and therefore we shall now discuss the sifting of true open clusters from agglomerates in field star distribution.

Lying among the rich star fields of the galactic plane, there are to be found groupings of stars which give the impression of being coarse open clusters. Such stellar concentrations are often logged by

Galactic Open Clusters.

amateurs, and even given personal designations. These asterisms stand out well in their respective fields in much the same way as some genuine open clusters of sparse membership, and a few are to be found in Norton's Star Atlas, erroneously plotted as bona-fide clusters.

The geometrical parameters of a cluster are useful; they define its shape, the numerical richness of its stars and their density gradient, and these alone will be enough to differentiate an open cluster from the great majority of globular clusters. Nevertheless, the physical characteristics of a cluster are also important, and these are defined by the chemical composition, age and luminosity function of the cluster stars. To extend knowledge of a cluster beyond its photographic appearance, therefore, detailed photometry and spectroscopy of its stars are needed.

In all branches of astronomy, it is natural that the brighter, larger objects will receive the maximum amount of attention. In the field of open clusters objects such as those in the Messier catalogue are well-studied, and detailed observations go back for many years. Other large, bright clusters not in Messier have also been subjected to the full range of observational procedures, but we still find that a large number of clusters are either only partially studied or not studied at all, apart from basic classification. In this context it is worth recalling that the first photometric observations of NGC 2420 did not take place until 1962. As well as relatively little-studied clusters in the NGC, there are also many more among the discoveries made by Ruprecht, Dolidze and others. Furthermore, with numbers of recently discovered clusters or possible clusters cropping up in the southern sky, the situation is unlikely to change for some time, bearing in mind the great amount of work required in order to study a cluster fully.

Luminosity Function of Open Clusters.

The luminosity function of a cluster is obtained by counting the number of stars in each magnitude interval or step, and this will differ from the luminosity function of a non-cluster field. In the latter case, the luminosity function is seen to increase with decreasing magnitude, while in the case of a true cluster the function shows a rise to the brighter cluster stars followed by a decrease to the fainter ones.

Figure 3 on page 12 shows the mean luminosity function of true open clusters compared with the apparent luminosity function of field stars. The differences are immediately apparent; the open clusters showing a mean maximum absolute magnitude of M_v =+5 while the field stars display maximum numbers at fainter apparent magnitudes. However, while the greater percentage of open clusters will show a luminosity function equivalent to Figure 3a, it is true to say that not necessarily all will do so.

12

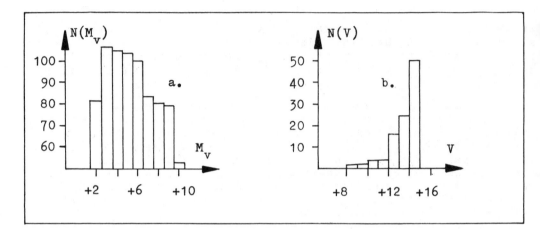

Figure 3. a, Mean luminosity function of real physical clusters
selected by van den Bergh (1961). b, Apparent luminosity function in the case of field stars.

4. Stellar Populations.

In the historical review we have seen that the concept of stellar
populations originated with Baade. Nowadays the scheme has been
elaborated, and comprises five population divisions, as can be seen
below in Table 2.

Table 2. Stellar Populations in the Galaxy.

Population Group	Type of Star	% of Metals.
Extreme Pop. II	Halo globular clusters	0.3
Intermediate Pop. II	RR Lyrae and halo stars	1.0
Disc Population	Main-sequence stars	2.0
Intermediate Pop. I	Old open clusters	3.0
Extreme Pop. I	Young open clusters	4.0
	O-B stars.	

From the above table it can be seen that there is a wide dispersion in metal abundance as a function of galactic latitude, and this
will be further discussed in Chapter 5 with regard to globular
clusters. As well as the metal-rich open clusters, Population I
regions of the Galaxy also contain classical Cepheid stars. These
variables are also to be found in some open clusters (e.g., UY Per
and VY Per in the Perseus Double Cluster, U Sgr in M25) and are
useful in deriving distances of the clusters in which they occur.
Further details of this will be found in Appendix 3.

Galactic Open Clusters.

5. Colour-Magnitude Diagrams.

The ability to cast light on the current evolutionary stage and age of a star cluster is the great function of a colour-magnitude diagram. The use of such a diagram is not confined to clusters alone, however; certain types of field stars are also subjected to such analysis, as well as luminous stars in nearby galaxies.

In contrast to star fields within the Galaxy, when we look at either an open or a globular cluster we are seeing stars which are of approximately the same age and with the same initial chemical composition. A colour-magnitude of a cluster is obtained by measuring the brightness of as many of its stars as possible in blue (B) and visual (V) wavelengths and then plotting V against B-V, the latter defining the star's colour. If stars in an open cluster are so plotted a well-defined locus is obtained, known as the main-sequence. In some clusters certain stars will form a region of the diagram known as the giant branch; in very young clusters this will be lacking while in old clusters it is more in evidence. While, as described above, the apparent magnitudes of cluster stars can be plotted on to a colour-magnitude diagram, to obtain data on the ages of clusters their distances are required in order that the apparent magnitudes can be converted into absolute magnitudes (M_V), which is the magnitude a star or any other object would display at a distance of 10 pc.

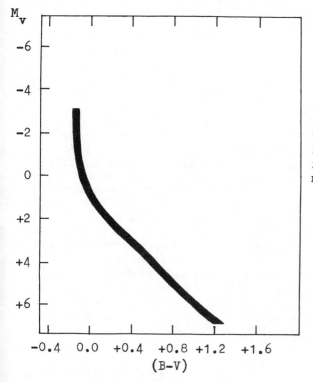

Figure 4. Colour-magnitude diagram for the Pleiades. The abscissa is the colour index (B-V), the ordinate is the absolute visual magnitude (M_V).

Galactic Open Clusters.

On the preceding page is shown a colour-magnitude diagram for the Pleiades. The band running from B-V = +1.2 to M_v = -3 is the cluster main-sequence; individually plotted cluster stars would basically lie along this line. It will be noted that there is no red giant branch for this cluster, which is indicative of its young age. The old open cluster M67 does, however, have a giant branch, as can be seen below in Figure 5.

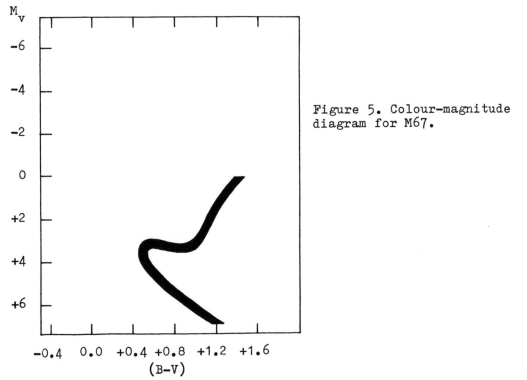

Figure 5. Colour-magnitude diagram for M67.

In stellar evolution, a proto-star will lie off to the right of the main-sequence. As the star evolves, it will eventually make contact with the main-sequence, the point where it does so being dependant upon its mass. A large mass star will make contact with the main-sequence at the upper left of the diagram, where stellar luminosities are high, while a small mass star will join the main-sequence at the lower right, and will hence be an object of low intrinsic luminosity. The locus of points at which stars of differing masses begin life on the main-sequence is referred to as the Zero Age Main Sequence (ZAMS). From then on the evolutionary track of a star is determined by its mass, the larger mass, high luminosity stars evolving more rapidly due to the high rate of their nuclear reactions. Although a star will spend the majority of its lifetime on the main-sequence, it will eventually move off to the upper right of the colour magnitude diagram as its nuclear reactions

Galactic Open Clusters.

undergo changes. The star, characterised by a larger angular size and red colour, is defined as a red giant, and many well-known stars are of this type, e.g., Antares, Aldebaran and Betelgeuse.

It can be seen from the above that the lower the turn-off point from the main-sequence the older the cluster. It is apparent, therefore, from Figures 4 and 5 that the Pleiades is a young cluster and that M67 is decidedly older in that it has a well-developed giant branch. Two further examples of well-known clusters, the Perseus Double Cluster and the Hyades, show this difference in a less extreme form; in the Perseus clusters the main-sequence is virtually intact, while the Hyades has already lost its blue stars to the giant branch.

The derivation of cluster ages also demands a good deal of theoretical work with which observations can be compared. Theoretical ZAMS models can be fitted to a sample of stars in a cluster in order to aid in age derivations, while calculations of the evolutionary tracks of stars from the ZAMS are also important. In the past, these theoretical evolutionary tracks for stars often agreed poorly with observed data plotted in the form of a colour-magnitude diagram, and current ages derived for clusters are well below these early figures; for example, an early derivation of the age of the open cluster NGC 188 was about $14\text{--}16 \times 10^9$ yr, while a recent figure by Hirshfeld, McClure and Twarog (1978) gives 5×10^9 yr as an age for this cluster. At the other end of the scale there is the Hyades, to which an age of only 0.7×10^9 yr has been assigned. For an even younger stellar group we can take the CMa R1 association, in which a number of hot stars are to be found illuminating nebulosity. In this association, which includes the emission-line stars Z CMa and HD 53367, no stars later than B5 are on the main-sequence, leading to a possible age for the group of only about 3×10^5 yr.

The derived age for the Pleiades is about 20×10^6 yr, but it is not one of the youngest clusters, the Perseus Double Cluster and NGC 2362 both being younger, the age of the latter being put at about one twentieth that of the Pleiades. Another young cluster is I39, where the majority of stars are still on the main-sequence, and just a few of the brightest are in the process of evolving towards the red giant stage.

A further consideration regarding cluster ages is that of metal abundance. Being relatively young objects, open clusters were formed at a stage in the evolution of the Galaxy when the interstellar material from which they coalesced was much richer than at earlier epochs, this being due to metal enrichment of the interstellar medium by successive generations of stars, each generation forming in a more metal-rich environment due to mass loss from earlier stars by various means, including supernova explosions. However, there is a significant spread in metal abundance in clusters of a given age, and hence interstellar material in the disc of the Galaxy, where clusters reside, has obviously been unevenly mixed during past epochs of galactic evolution. Older open clusters such

Galactic Open Clusters.

as NGC 2420 and NGC 2506 show a degree of metal deficiency. These two
clusters, along with others, lie in the region of the galactic anti-
centre, and 2 to 4 kpc from the galactic nucleus. Data on metal
deficiency for a large number of clusters now indicates that with
increasing distance from the galactic centre, clusters show a decrease
in metal abundance, and that for about the last 5×10^9 yr the position
of a cluster in the Galaxy determines its metal content, and not the
cluster age.

Finally we come to the the question of the stability of open
clusters, or, to put it another way, over what period of time is a
cluster liable to retain its identity as a unit? For a cluster to be
stable, its internal gravitation must exceed the tidal forces of the
parent galaxy, and to do this it must have a density greater than a
specific figure. We can arrive at this figure by multiplying the mass
of the Galaxy by 10 and dividing it by the cube of the distance
between the two relevant centroids, that of the Galaxy and that of th
cluster. From such computations it can be demonstrated that all those
clusters which have star densities less than one star per $10 \, pc^3$ are
very unstable, and will therefore be quickly disrupted by galactic
tidal forces. In the Pleiades, the central density is about 0.1 star
per pc^3, which makes these regions fairly stable, although not by a
large amount. The density of stars in the Hyades is about one quarter
of the Pleiades figure, and the degree of instability is thus much
greater. On a time scale of about 2×10^9 yr about half of the origin
stars in a cluster will have dispersed owing to tidal forces and the
perturbations of nearby stars, and this adds further weight to our
knowledge that open clusters are young objects. From this it can be
seen that many clusters which once existed have now broken up, and
that their constituent stars have dispersed within the star fields
of the Galaxy.

3. CATALOGUES OF OPEN CLUSTERS.

The list of open clusters that the great majority of amateurs are familiar with is that contained in the Atlas Coeli catalogue, which gives details of 243 clusters over the whole sky. Two of these, however, are erroneously catalogued globular clusters, NGC 6558 and NGC 6642. From the point of view of this volume, which has (with a few exceptions) a declination limit of −30°, Coeli lists 187 open clusters. This gives a large and varied sample, but by no means exhausts the number of clusters available to the visual observer, many of the omitted clusters being of equal or greater interest than those plotted on the Coeli charts.

With Coeli as the standard amateur reference, it is instructive to look at the source from which the Coeli open clusters were taken. This is the catalogue of 249 clusters compiled by Shapley in 1930, and while it was a great advance on earlier lists such as that of Melotte (162 clusters) it cannot be classed as comprehensive for the present day observer. Since Shapley's catalogue appeared, many new clusters have been sifted from the rich star fields of the Galaxy, while any early problems in classification have in general been settled. The list of open clusters in Coeli is, therefore, to a certain extent limited by the epoch of its source material. Furthermore, Coeli does not include 16 bright clusters which are to be found plotted in Norton's Star Atlas, and these are shown below in Table 3.

Table 3. Bright Open Clusters Omitted from Coeli.

NGC 136	NGC 2331
225	2343
381	2374
1444	2395
1778	2396
2232	6568
2251	6800
2286	7082

For a comprehensive catalogue of all types of clusters we must refer to the Catalogue of Star Clusters, Associations and Groups, first published in 1958, second edition 1970. Nine supplements appeared between the two editions, in which Helen Sawyer Hogg collaborated with other compilers. The material contained in these supplements was incorporated in the 1970 edition, while more recent material will appear in a third edition.

This catalogue comprises data and references for 1039 open clusters, 5 moving clusters and 11 star groups, the information being presented on 1185 cards. Also included are 86 cards with data on 70 associations plus further cards on globular clusters.

Of the 1039 open clusters in this publication, over 700 are not

Catalogues of Open Clusters

NGC or IC objects, and of these only 27 are to be found in Coeli. This leaves a large residue which can be fruitfully employed by the amateur and while many of these clusters are not particularly interesting in a visual sense, many will be found to be challenging objects for the majority of amateur telescopes. A few of these clusters, observed with a 10-inch telescope, appear in the catalogue in Part 2 of this volume, while a selection of others is given in the list of additional objects

The number of known clusters has increased considerably since Helen Sawyer Hogg compiled a list of over 500 in 1959. Currently many newly-discovered probable groups are emerging from surveys in the southern hemisphere. Some of these appear very like asterisms, being of sparse membership and loose structure, and only detailed study will eventuall disclose their true nature. The following references give details of a few of these more recent discoveries.

Loden, L.O.	1973, Astron. & Astrophys. Supp. 10, 125-133. (44 clusters in the Car-Cen regions).
Moffat, A.F.J. Vogt, N.	1975, Astron. & Astrophys. Supp. 20, 85-153. (11 previously uncatalogued clusters).
Van den Bergh, S.	1975, Astron. J. 80, 11-16. (63 uncatalogued clusters).
Loden, L.O.	1979, Astron. & Astrophys. Supp. 36, 83-93. (Loose clusters in the S. Milky Way).

4. OBSERVATION OF OPEN CLUSTERS.

INTRODUCTION.

When consideration is taken of the wide dispersion in angular sizes shown by open clusters, plus their varied morphology and range of observable stars, it can be seen that all sizes of telescopes used by amateurs, as well as binoculars, are catered for. A number of clusters of lesser size and brightness than the Pleiades, Hyades, M44 and the Perseus Double Cluster can be naked-eye objects in a good sky, while binoculars will increase the number substantially, although in many instances adequate resolution will not be obtained.

To do full justice to open clusters, large telescopes (by amateur standards) are not required, an aperture of 8 to 10-inches, in a good location, being perfectly suitable. Certainly a telescope of either of these sizes is not only ideal for study of a considerable number of NGC and IC clusters, but is also useful for extending observations to include objects that are either little-known or completely unknown to many amateurs. As the contents of the present catalogue will show, a number of the latter have been successfully observed with a 10-inch reflector, while a further selection of such clusters will be found in the list of additional objects.

The chapter is divided into two sections: 1. Identification of open clusters and 2. Cluster characteristics, the latter including passages on unresolved stars, associated nebulosity and star colours. Details will also be given on the two brightest flare stars in the Pleiades, a cluster which is rich in these objects.

1. Identification of Open Clusters.

The problems inherent in correct identification of many clusters are not only related to those of small angular diameter and faint stellar membership; large, quite rich clusters can also present identification problems when they are associated with rich fields. Equally difficult can be clusters of sparse membership inhabiting similar fields. Chance alignments of stars (asterisms) can also be misleading, and, often lacking the facilities to check results against such publications as the Palomar Sky Survey or Vehrenberg's Atlas Stellarum, the observer is left to make the best he can of uncertain observations.

Reference photographs of clusters are a great asset; unfortunately those photographs that usually appear in books and journals are invariably of the brighter, well-known objects, impossible to mistake at the eyepiece. In some cases photographs of other clusters are to be found in professional journals, and a list of these, plus other publications, will be found in Appendix

The Palomar Sky Survey prints are very useful for checking observations, but not only are those copies which are housed in professional institutions unavailable to most amateurs, their purchase is an expensive (although rewarding) business. The Palomar prints have a limiting magnitude of over 20 mag, and large numbers of open clusters appear prominently. In certain cases, however, a cluster will

Observation of Open Clusters.

lie in a region of particularly rich star distribution, or be heavily
swamped in emission nebulosity, and in such cases it is often difficult
to define the cluster. A suitable example is Cr 428; visually this
cluster appears as a loosely-structured object showing no great degree
of stellar concentration. Loose as it is, however, it does stand out
visually in a moderate telescope. The same cannot be said of the image
of this cluster on the Sky Survey. On the red (E) print Cr 428 is
totally swamped by the great expanse of the North American Nebula, while
even on the blue (O) print, there is no real indication of a cluster due
to heavy contamination by field stars. Numbers of visually observed
stars can, however, be identified.

Identical in many ways is Dol 5. Again field stars overpower the
cluster, although not to such an extent as in the previous case. Some
stars observed visually can be identified, but on the Sky Survey print
the fields to the W of Dol 5 are virtually of equal density to the
cluster region. Furthermore, bright and dark nebulosity of quite high
intensity criss-crosses the cluster neighbourhood.

In many cases good correlation can be achieved between visual and
photographic appearance. On the Sky Survey small, compressed clusters
such as Mark 50 present photographic images that differ but little from
their visual appearance. Without citing further examples, it can be
said that comparisons of this kind are very satisfying, showing as they
do just how much detail can be resolved in many clusters with telescope
of moderate aperture.

Due to their proximity to the solar system, a few open clusters appe
to be situated well away from the boundaries of the galactic plane. For
northern hemisphere observers the prime examples are M44, M45 and the
Coma cluster (Mel 111). These are, of course, naked-eye objects, as are
some other Messier clusters and the Perseus Double Cluster, even though
these latter appear within the band of the Milky Way. Many other groups
stand out well in their neighbourhoods when seen through telescopes,
but others are heavily affected by local star distribution, particularl
those clusters in which the stars are loosely spread. In such cases the
field stars can pretty well overpower a cluster, and even some rich
objects can be heavily affected. At the other extreme we find clusters
located in regions of dark nebulosity, which are visually apparent by
a paucity of field stars. Such regions are advantageous, either fully
blanketing, or effectively dimming, numbers of field stars and thereby
reducing their contamination of a given cluster.

2. Cluster Characteristics.

Due to the irregular morphology of open clusters, their structural
characteristics are of great variety, and often reveal sub-groups of
stars as well as double and multiple groupings within the overall image
First among the points we shall cover here is that of overall structure

Overall structure of Clusters.

There is no better introduction to the structural variations display
by open clusters than that furnished by the 27 objects of this type in
the Messier catalogue. These range from clusters of loose concentration
such as M29 to compressed, rich objects such as M11. The differences

Observation of Open Clusters.

apparent in clusters of identical Shapley type will be a function of distance. Thus, if we take two clusters of Shapley class 'e', M7 and M52, their respective distances of about 250 and 925 pc will greatly affect their telescopic appearance. Being the nearer of the two, M7 virtually fills a 1° field; in contrast M52 is only about 20 arcminutes in greatest angular size, and therefore appears more cluster-like, the angular separation of its stars being considerably reduced.

The boundaries of open clusters are often fairly well-defined, and for many objects an overall elongation will be seen. This will be primarily due to the effects of galactic rotation, and thus the major axes of many clusters will show a tendency to be aligned to a certain extent parallel to the galactic plane. However, it appears that this relation of major axis to galactic plane does not always operate, and differences of this kind may be related in some measure to cluster ages.

Variations in the overall structure of clusters will become more apparent as the large numbers of objects outside of the Messier clusters are encountered, and we can do no better than refer to the observations in the accompying catalogue for these variations to be appreciated.

Magnitudes of Open Clusters.

Integrated magnitude figures are not available for all clusters, and in particular have not been determined for many objects of relatively recent discovery. For the majority of NGC and IC objects, however, magnitudes are available. The 27 clusters in the Messier catalogue have a dispersion of almost 6 magnitudes, the lower limit being 7.5 mag for M18. When we consider clusters outside the Messier objects, there is inevitably a concentration towards much fainter magnitudes. In the catalogue of open clusters in this Handbook the majority of objects are in the 9 to 10 magnitude range.

Magnitude figures, however, do not give a meaningful indication of the visual appearance of a cluster. While the magnitudes of cluster stars are important, other contributory factors are the distribution of the stars and the character of the cluster area, the latter having already been discussed above. Only for very small clusters where, due to the effects of distance, the component stars are closely grouped, will a magnitude figure have much of a bearing, and even then not a great deal. The magnitudes which are of interest to observers, therefore, are not the integrated ones, but those of cluster stars.

The Range of Cluster Stars.

With the intrinsic magnitudes of some cluster stars peaking at about $M_v = -5$, the nearest clusters in which such stars are present will display members of quite high visual magnitudes. The brightest star in the Pleiades, for example, has $m_v = 2.96$, and even in a fainter, more distant cluster such as M44 the brightest stars are of about mv =6.0, while the brightest members of other clusters in

Observation of Open Clusters.

the Messier list are often seen to reach $m_v = 8.0$. As we shall see, the magnitudes of many cluster stars eventually become too faint to register in moderate telescopes as individual points, but where a number of them are concentrated together they give the appearance of a region of nebulosity.

In cases where closely grouped, faint stars show as nebulosity, the observer is not in a position to state whether these nebulous regions are due to unresolved stars or are actual emission regions. In most cases the former will be the case, and concentrated observation in good seeing will often reveal a small number of faint stars within the nebulous area. A number of such cases occur in the observations used in this Handbook, and we have examined a few on the Sky Survey prints. In some instances the nebulous regions were actually regions of emission, and these will be discussed later, in those cases where the nebulosity was due to unresolved stars we have selected two for comment.

The two clusters in question are NGC 6819 and Tr 9. In both of these nebulous regions were observed with a 10-inch reflector; the region in NGC 6819 being horseshoe-like in shape, that in Tr 9 being structureless. Comparison of the drawings of the clusters with the Sky Survey images showed that in both cases the nebulous regions are composed of unresolved stars, the concentration being heaviest in NGC 6819.

Finally, we take the question of the number of stars to be seen in clusters. Counts of these are often made by visual observers, and this raises the point of true cluster membership, a point which is enhanced in those instances where clusters inhabit rich fields, and a merging of cluster and field stars occurs.

As the derivation of true cluster stars is by no means an easy task for the professional astronomer, it can be appreciated that exact determination of them is beyond amateur capabilities. The fainter cluster stars are beyond visual observation, and definition of any brighter ones can be highly uncertain. The most that the visual observer can achieve in this sphere, therefore, is to give an indication of the number of stars that appear to be within the confines of a given cluster down to whatever limiting magnitude can can be reached. Occasionally a cluster will be encountered which is located in a relatively barren field, and here a more definitive result may be obtained with star counts.

It may legitimately be thought that the given angular diameter of a cluster can be used to fix its boundaries, but this is not the case. Angular diameters of a cluster can vary widely, depending upon the source, while true membership of many clusters is still a long way from being finalised.

Clusters Associated with Nebulosity.

In many clusters nebulous regions are not indicative of unresolved stars but consist of actual nebulosity, and this can vary considerably in size and brightness. In many cases the nebulosity is quite small in apparent dimensions while at the other extreme it is very extended and

Observation of Open Clusters.

either fairly bright or very faint. In associations such as
M8 and M16 the nebulosity can be observed without difficulty
from mid-northern latitudes, and a fair amount of detail can
be made out.

It is natural to associate nebulosity, whether connected
with clusters or not, with the rich regions lying towards the
galactic centre, and certainly such associations are bright
objects. There are, however, plenty of clusters immersed in
emission nebulosity in the anti-centre regions of the Galaxy,
and these are always worth while observing, as in the dark
winter skies which these associations frequent, some signs of
nebulosity may be apparent in suitable telescopes, a rich-
field telescope possibly registering some of the more extended
nebulosity in the region of clusters like Mel 15, where the
emission nebula is IC 1805.

A good example of a cluster involved with large areas of
nebulosity is NGC 7380. Here both bright and dark nebulosity
is strikingly apparent on photographs, and what appears to
be some of the former is recorded in the relevant entry in
the catalogue of clusters in Part Three.

A further small group of clusters in which nebulosity was
suspected have been examined on the Palomar prints. NGC 2174
and 2175, NGC 2467 and NGC 6910 are the clusters, all were
found to be associated with emission, and the observed areas
of nebulosity corresponded well with the images on the prints.
For all its general faintness, nebulosity connected with
clusters is well worth searching for, and for this reason we
list in the catalogue any cluster with nebulosity connected
or in the general region, although we have omitted cases in
which the intensity level of the emission is too low for
visual observation.

Star Colours and Flare Stars.

Although the magnitudes of most cluster stars are too faint
for much in the way of colour to be seen, some colour is
noticeable in certain cases. Individual examples are to be
found in the catalogue, but in passing we can mention examples
in the Perseus Double Cluster, where at the respective centres
are to be seen numbers of red and blue stars within quite small
regions, and which present an impressive spectacle.

Flare stars are to be found in many clusters; of the UV Cet
type, they appear in NGC 2264, M42 and the Taurus dark clouds.
Many, such as V371 Ori, are sources of radio emission, but
unfortunately the majority reach very low magnitudes even at
maximum. Two, however, in the Pleiades come within reach of
amateur telescopes, and details are shown overleaf in Table 4,
while Figure 6, also overleaf, shows a chart of the Pleiades
with the positions of the flare stars plotted.

Observation of Open Clusters.

Table 4. Flare Stars in the Pleiades.

	(1950)			
Star	RA	Dec	Spec	Max
A	03 42.6	+23 29	dK5e	13.4
B	03 43.4	+24 30	K7	13.3

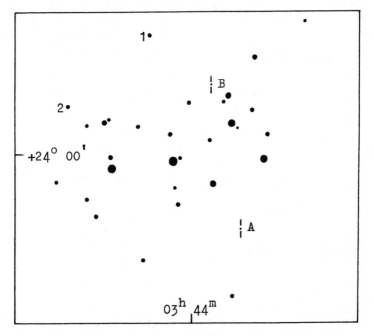

Figure 6. 30 stars in the Pleiades field to magnitude V = 7.54. Stars 1 and 2 are not members, and the positions of the two flare stars are marked A and B.

PART TWO : GLOBULAR CLUSTERS.

HISTORICAL REVIEW.

There was no category of celestial object recognised as globular clusters until Wm. Herschel first used the description in his catalogues of nebulae of 1786, and even there the description does not always match the distinction we apply today.

We now know that omega Centauri is a globular cluster, but to ancient observers it was considered a single star - hence its enumeration as omega by Bayer in his Uranometria of 1603. The first recognition of this object as a 'nebula' (or 'lucid spot like a cloud') was due to Halley who examined it telescopically at St. Helena in 1677, and it was also Halley who in 1714 first discovered M13 in Hercules, which he described as 'but a little Patch, but it shows itself to the Naked Eye when the Sky is serene and the Moon absent'.

However, the first globular cluster to be discovered as a 'nebula' was not found by Halley, but by the German, Abraham Ihle, who came upon M22 in Sagittarius, apparently by accident while observing Saturn in 1665. Between the dates of Halley's two globular cluster discoveries another was found by Gottfried Kirch in 1702; this was M5 in Serpens. It was not until 1745 that the tally of globulars was raised to six, when de Chésaux came upon M4 in Scorpio (which he described as 'small, white and round') and M71 in Sagitta. The next year, 1746, saw the addition of two more globulars, M2 in Aquarius and M15 in Pegasus, both being picked up by the French astronomer Maraldi while looking for de Chésaux' comet of 1746.

During his expedition to the Cape of Good Hope in 1751-52, the Abbé Lacaille added five new globulars to the known total, these being NGC 104 (47 Toucani), NGC 4833, NGC 6397, M69 and M55. The contribution of Messier to the gathering of new globular clusters is impressive: he began by picking up eight: M3, M9, M10, M12, M14, M19, M28, M30, between 3rd May and 3rd August 1764, and thereafter he and Méchain between them contributed another ten by March 1781.

As described in the Historical Review of Open Clusters, the phenomenal gathering of nebulae by the elder Herschel brought many more globular clusters into view, but a more definitive analysis had to await the invention of the spectroscope and its application to astronomy by pioneers like Wm. Huggins, and the classification of stellar spectra by Secchi. Further progress followed the recognition of RR Lyrae variable stars in globular clusters by S.I. Bailey in 1900, the introduction of the Hertzsprung-Russell diagram in 1905, and, in 1917, the derivation of the distance of the solar system to the nucleus of the Galaxy by Shapley. For this distance determination (now much revised) Shapley made a study of the distribution of globulars, noting their preponderance in the Sco-Oph-Sgr regions of the sky, where, obscured by dark nebulae, the nucleus of the Galaxy is situated.

Historical Review.

Further impetus was gained in the study of globular clusters by Walter Baade's analysis of stellar populations in 1944. Since then, due primarily to the large-scale plates of the Sky Survey, further globular clusters have been identified within the Galaxy, while plates taken by large reflectors have revealed many of these objects in external galaxies.

5. GALACTIC GLOBULAR CLUSTERS.

INTRODUCTION.

With globular clusters we are concerned with objects that are of high intrinsic luminosity, great age and, in contrast to open clusters, do not show space distribution that is largely concentrated to the galactic plane.

While open clusters are known in external galaxies, globular clusters are much more numerous in this context, and in those cases where globulars are suitable for detailed study, are very useful for comparison with clusters in the Galaxy. These extragalactic globular clusters will be covered in more detail in Chapter 6.

The study of globular clusters takes us back to the early evolutionary stages of the Galaxy, and, among other things, information derived from studies of globulars is of importance in that knowledge of the early chemical composition of the Galaxy can be obtained. This chapter will be concerned with the various properties of globular clusters, beginning with classification and concluding with colour-magnitude diagrams and cluster ages. From the point of view of space, coverage of these aspects must of necessity be brief, but hopefully an adequate picture of these objects will be portrayed.

1. Classification.

The only classification of globular clusters that most amateurs will be familiar with is that of Shapley, and as this is purely a structural scheme, it is of use to visual observers. Details of other classifications will be given below.

Shapley's classification is based upon the degree of concentration shown by cluster stars, and is divided into twelve classes, ranging from Class I - the most highly concentrated, to Class XII - the lowest concentration. This scheme shows the wide range of star distribution in globular clusters, and, as will be shown in Chapter 8, concentration class, along with other factors, has a considerable bearing upon results obtained by visual observers. Also affected by these structural properties are matters relating to the discovery of globular clusters on photographs taken by large telescopes.

In astronomy, classification of objects is nowadays not always a structure-related procedure. We have only to think of Seyfert galaxies in this context; initially the classification was purely structural, but is now seen as a spectroscopic concept. Spectroscopic classification can relate considerably to differences in chemical content between different classes of object, and this is seen in the field of globular clusters. A classification scheme for globulars has been developed by W.W. Morgan, and this is based upon the integrated spectrum of a cluster. The scheme runs from I through to VIII, the former indicating a cluster with very weak metallic spectral lines, the latter a cluster whose spectrum

Galactic Globular Clusters

shows the strongest metallicity. The usefulness of Morgan's method
bears directly upon the probable variations in cluster formation
during the early evolution of the Galaxy.

It has been known for some time that those stars in the Galaxy
whose spectra show a high metal content are young objects. Older
objects, among which are included globular clusters, are all known
to be metal-poor, this being a product of their formation in the
early epochs of galactic evolution, at a time when the interstellar
medium had not been enriched by heavier elements formed in stellar
interiors and dispersed by various means back into space. However,
spectroscopy of globular clusters showed that differences occuring
in cluster spectra could not be reconciled with such a simple
statement as old = metal-poor. From this Morgan's classification
evolved. These variations in cluster spectra indicate differences
in cluster formation as a function of galactic latitude, viz., the
clusters at low galactic latitudes show spectra of higher metal
content than those at higher galactic latitudes. A likely explanation
of this is that the low latitude clusters may be the result of
quicker star formation and thus higher metal enrichment of the
interstellar medium. A similar classification of globular clusters
is the Deutsch-Kinman system: A = medium metal abundance; B = low
metal abundance and C = very low metal abundance.

Globular clusters are also divided into Oosterhoff groups, a
scheme which divides clusters into two classes and is based upon
the types of RR Lyrae variable stars in a given cluster. In these
clusters RR Lyrae stars are of two types: RRc variables have periods
of less than 0.4 days and have small amplitudes; RRab variables show
periods of over 0.4 days and have amplitudes up to 1.7 mag. RRc
variables are on average bluer objects than RRab's. The clusters are
divided into two groups according to the number and mean period of
their RRc and RRab variables. In Group I RRab stars are present in
larger numbers than RRc stars while in Group II RRc stars are twice
as numerous as RRab's. Examples of Oosterhoff Group I clusters are
M3, M5 and NGC 6229, while Oosterhoff Group II clusters number among
them M2, M15 and NGC 5466. In passing it is worth mentioning that
90% of known cluster variables are RR Lyrae stars, and that clusters
rich in these mainly belong to the halo population of clusters in
the Galaxy, objects of low metal abundance.

2. Relation of Globular Clusters to the Galaxy.

If one looks at a plot of globular clusters in a star atlas,
and compares this with the distribution of open clusters, the
differences are immediately apparent. The globulars inhabit the
central and halo regions of the Galaxy, and the dispersion in z is
correspondingly extreme. Lower figures for globular clusters show
z = 0.1 and upper figures z = +64. In Figure 7 overleaf, the
distribution in the Galaxy of 129 globular clusters is shown, these
being taken from the catalogue of Kukarkin (1974). In the diagram
the concentration of clusters at the centre of the Galaxy is well-

seen, and it is in these regions that the the full effects of heavy
obscuration by interstellar matter is most pronounced. Studies of
the regions of individual clusters show considerable absorption, but
at least these clusters register in visible wavelengths, for there
are some clusters that do not. Within an area defined by galactic
latitude +1.7 to -2.7, galactic longitude 8.4 to 356.0, are to be
found a number of extremely obscured clusters, these being so
reddened due to absorption that they are detectable only in the
infrared. These clusters, detected by Terzan, are quite recent
additions to the ranks of galactic globular clusters.

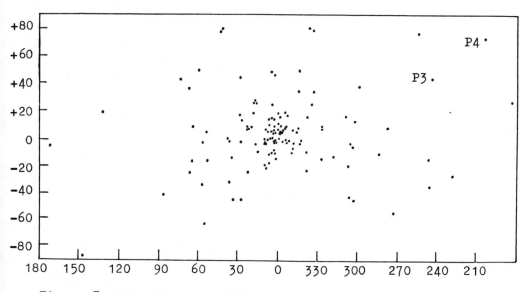

Figure 7. Galactic distribution of 129 globular clusters. The
Palomar clusters Pal. 3 and Pal. 4 are indicated on the chart.

3. Structure of Globular Clusters.

The morphology of 'classical' globular clusters, exemplified by
objects such as M13 and omega Cen, is familiar to the amateur.
The majority of the Messier clusters are of Concentration Class V,
while the lowest class for these clusters is M55, with a Concentration Class of XI, and being of such loose structure is easily
resolved with moderate telescopes, and even on photographs the
difference in structure of this cluster, when compared with the
more heavily concentrated clusters, is clear.

Out of the 130 odd globular clusters known in the Galaxy, there
are eleven of Concentration Class XII, and of these seven are among
the clusters discovered on the Palomar Sky Survey plates. These
clusters display structure very different from objects of the M13
ilk, being of very low density, so low, in fact, that they would

Galactic Globular Clusters.

be disrupted by galactic tidal forces if they made too close an approach. Such clusters, lying well out in the galactic halo, are exemplified by Palomar 3 and Palomar 4, which are marked on the chart on page 29.

All of the halo globular clusters, objects with large z, have large intrinsic diameters, Palomar 3, for example, having an actual diameter of 61 pc. Compare this with clusters of small z, such as NGC 6838 (z = -0.2) which has an intrinsic diameter of only 6 pc. The reason for this is that galactic tidal forces limit the radii of most clusters, and if these forces are small a given cluster will show a larger intrinsic diameter. The radii shown by distant Palomar clusters in the galactic halo are explained if they have never come closer than 9000 pc to the galactic centre.

The integrated photographic magnitudes of Palomar clusters are of the order of 15 mag, yet they are by no means easy to detect. The reason for this is their lack of stellar concentration, and hence their inability to stand out in distant star fields. Objects such as M3 and M13 are more populous in stars by a factor of 10 than are the halo Palomar clusters. Six of the latter are barely recognisable on the Sky Survey plates; all are of Concentration Class XII and lie in regions unaffected by galactic obscuration.

4. Colour-Magnitude Diagrams.

We have seen in Part One (Table 2) that halo globular clusters form the extreme Population II regions of the Galaxy; this shows them to be extremely old objects, with ages of the order of about 10^{10} yr.

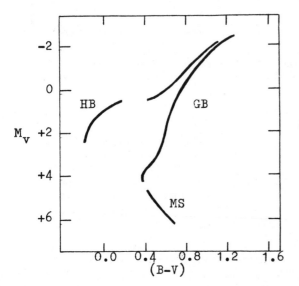

Figure 8. C-M diagram for M15. MS refers to the main-sequence, HB the horizontal branch and GB the giant branch.

Galactic Globular Clusters.

Figure 8 shows a colour-magnitude diagram for the cluster M15, and the difference between this and the diagram shown for the Pleiades on page 13 is immediately apparent. Note the position of the main-sequence turn-off point for M15 at M_v +4, which is indicative of its old age, for as we have seen, the lower the turn-off point the older the cluster. Comparison of the M15 diagram with that for M67 on page 14 shows some similarities; both clusters having lost stars to the giant branch. For determination of cluster ages the luminosities and temperatures of stars both on and below the turn-off are necessary, plus distances and metal abundances. Also required are theoretical evolutionary tracks for stars of the necessary chemical composition and mass.

With photoelectrically determined colours of cluster stars, which are a measure of stellar temperature, metal content of stars derived from their spectra and computed theoretical models, a great amount of data can be collected. However, many problems exist in the aquisition of such information, in particular that of deriving accurate magnitudes for faint cluster members. In addition, the process of photometry is often rendered difficult due to the effects of crowding by other stars, particularly in those cases where the photometry is undertaken close to the centre of a cluster.

Evolution of Globular Cluster Stars.

At first sight the colour-magnitude diagram for M15 on page 30 appears rather anomalous; a turn-off point is visible, and yet there are still luminous stars to the upper left of the turn-off. In order to explain this we shall now define the processes through which stars in a globular cluster pass in order to register on such a colour-magnitude diagram as shown in Figure 8.

The greater part of a star's lifetime is spent on the main-sequence, and we now wish to know the evolutionary sequence from the moment when a star leaves the main-sequence and moves into the giant branch region of a colour-magnitude diagram. The regions of the diagram we shall be concerned with are the horizontal branch and the asymptotic branch, which is shown immediately above the giant branch in Figure 8.

Upon leaving the main-sequence, a star will spend about 10^9 yr on the subgiant branch, which lies below the giant branch. During this period hydrogen undergoes nuclear reactions which transform it into helium, this occuring in a shell surrounding the core of the star, which at this time comprises inert helium. Following this phase, an almost identical period of time is spent on the giant branch.

Eventually a star will reach a period in its evolution where it will appear at the uppermost point of the giant branch. At this point the helium in the core begins burning, an event known as the 'helium flash'. While these reactions are taking place, the star will switch position on the colour-magnitude diagram and appear on the horizontal branch. Its position in this part of the diagram will depend upon the

Galactic Globular Clusters.

amount of mass it has lost during the red giant phase; the greater the mass loss, the bluer the position it will attain on the horizontal branch.

Once the helium in the star's core has been consumed. it will leave the horizontal branch, having spent a little less time there than on the giant branch. The star's next move is to appear on the asymptotic branch of the diagram, its position here once again being determined by its mass.

A star on the asymptotic branch is a very old object, and it is very likely that a star in the upper reaches of the asymptotic branch may undergo a phase of thermal instability, and hence lose a considerable percentage of its mass. In Volume 2 of this series it was described how planetary nebulae may evolve from red giant or supergiant stars, and in this context it has been shown by theory that the result of the thermal instability of an asymptotic branch star may be pulsations analogous to those that occur in Mira—type variable stars. During this process, the majority of material lying above the hydrogen shell of a star may be ejected, and it is possible that this process may result in the form-ation of a planetary nebula.

Planetary nebulae are not known to be numerous in globular clusters up until quite recently, in fact, only one was known to be associated with a cluster, Ps 1 in M15. Lately, however, it has been shown that there may be a second planetary in M15, and it is possible that it may be associated with an X-ray source thought to lie at the centre of the cluster. In 1977 a planetary was found about 3 arcminutes away from the globular cluster NGC 6401, and that it is possibly a cluster member.

X-Ray and Radio Sources in Globular Clusters.

A number of globular clusters show evidence of X-ray emission, among them NGC 6440, NGC 6441 and, as mentioned above, M15. These sources may indicate that globular clusters of high concentration have managed to retain some gas, although currently the mechanism responsible for the X-ray emission is not certain. One idea put forward is that of the existence of black holes at the centres of X-ray clusters.

Some globular clusters are known to have radio sources in their respective fields, and while it is possible that these sources may be associated with the clusters, it is also possible that they may be extragalactic in origin. Among the radio globulars are some of the Messier objects, including M2, M3 and M92. In the latter two cases the radio sources are similar to those exhibited by certain planetary nebulae, and thus it is possible that more planetaries associated with globular clusters await discovery optically. At the present time, however, nothing is definite in this field.

6. GLOBULAR CLUSTERS IN EXTERNAL GALAXIES.

Being objects of high intrinsic luminosity, globular clusters
are detectable out to considerable distances. We therefore find
them not only associated with galaxies in the Local Group, but also
with large elliptical galaxies in clusters such as the Virgo and
Hydra II clusters. Such extra-galactic globular clusters are of
importance, as they can be utilised to derive such information as
the masses of giant galaxies, and the distance moduli of galaxy
clusters.

Most amateurs are probably familiar with photographs of the
giant E galaxy M87, and have noted the great swarm of globular
clusters distributed around its outer regions. Other bright, E-
type galaxies in the Virgo cluster of galaxies are seen to be very
rich in globulars, in particular NGC's 4374, 4406, 4472, 4486 and
4647/4649. Rich in globular clusters as these are, the sum total
of their globular cluster population is a little over half the
number of globulars in M87. Where the parent galaxy is an E-type,
i.e., red, as in the above examples, a suitable plate/filter
combination is necessary, in order to reduce contamination by
galaxy material. In Figure 9 we show the distribution of 60
clusters around the Virgo Cluster galaxy NGC 4216; the dispersion
in magnitudes of these clusters is quite large, the brightest
cluster having a magnitude of 17.46 and the faintest a magnitude
of 22.84. The differences in brightness of the clusters is not
shown in the figure.

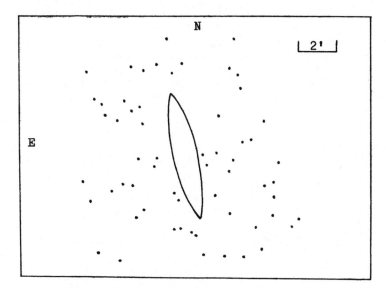

Figure 9. Distribution of 60 globular
clusters in NGC 4216.

Globular Clusters in External Galaxies.

Coming now to the Local Group of galaxies, we find that globular clusters are associated with a wide variety of galaxy types, ranging from the Fornax dwarf galaxy to M31. In particular, many globulars are connected with the Magellanic Clouds, numbers of these being NGC objects, and the brightnesses of these clusters are such that they have been the subject of Colour-Magnitude diagrams by Arp, Woolley and others. Examples of fairly loose globular clusters are also to be found in the Magellanic Clouds, objects such as LW 441 and LW 467 However, in these and other cases, the level of detectability is greater than for the Palomar clusters, and it must be remembered tha some of the latter are possibly at greater distances than the two Magellanic Clouds.

One difference between globular clusters in the Galaxy and those in the Magellanic Clouds is that the latter harbour blue, apparently young, clusters with lower age limits of about 5×10^6 yr. Some of these young clusters have a stellar content similar to open clusters in the Galaxy, objects such the Perseus Double Cluster and the Pleiades. Study of these clusters in the Magellanic Clouds is deemed important due to the fact that they can give an insight into the conditions in which globular clusters can form. Such conditions are extant in the Magellanic Clouds, but not, of course, in the Galaxy itself.

Briefly we shall now consider other globular clusters associated with Local Group galaxies, and at this point we take leave of the clusters with NGC designations, apart from the isolated instance of NGC 1049, the brightest cluster in the Fornax dwarf galaxy.

NGC 147 and NGC 185 have small retinues of globular clusters, ranging from diffuse objects to more compact, higher surface brightness objects. A solitary cluster lies on the west border of the Wolf-Lundmark-Melotte (WLM) galaxy. For the largest numbers of clusters associated with a Local Group galaxy, we turn, inevitably one feels, to M31. Currently a search for new clusters is in progress, and to date has yielded a large number. Early searches for M31 clusters, however, go back to Hubble's observations of 1932.

M31 is a massive galaxy, as is M87, and both are rich in globular clusters. It now appears that globular cluster membership of a galaxy is a function of galaxy mass; hence all massive galaxies should play host to a considerable number of clusters. The foregoing, by implication, shows that galaxy type is unrelated to cluster numbers, and in this context we have only to recall the large numbers of clusters associated with massive galaxies in the Virgo Cluster, in particular M87, where the number of clusters known is very high, being of the order of 2000.

7. CATALOGUES OF GLOBULAR CLUSTERS.

Early catalogues of globular clusters registered a fairly high percentage of those that are currently known; Melotte's list of 1915 showed 83 clusters, and by 1930 Shapley had compiled comprehensive data for 93 objects. In this catalogue, Shapley considered 7 of the listed objects as doubtful, but currently these are all considered to be globular clusters, and include NGC 1651, a cluster in the Small Magellanic Cloud.

In Chapter 3, we have remarked that correct classification of most clusters is, at first sight, a simple matter, assuming that the only criteria is that of morphology. This, however, is not a valid method, denying, as it does, the all-important factor of the stellar content of clusters. Over the years difficulties in classification have, in general, been resolved. For example, Shapley was undecided whether to to class NGC 2477 as the richest open cluster or the loosest globular, but currently this object is listed as the former type of object. A further example is NGC 2158, once thought to be a probable globular, but now seen as an open cluster. The stellar content of NGC 2158 is similar to that of NGC 752, but morphologically the two clusters are poles apart. In the 1960's a supposed globular cluster, known as the 'Russian Cluster', was studied, and finally turned out to be a distant cluster of Galaxies.

The three main catalogues of globular clusters which have appeared over the last 15 years are those of Arp (1965), Alcaino (1973) and Kukarkin (1974). The number of clusters listed in these varies between 119 and 131. In his catalogue of galactic globular clusters Arp includes NGC 1841, which is now classed as a member of the Magellanic Cloud system. Also, when Arp compiled his catalogue, a number of heavily obscured clusters, detectable only in the infrared, had yet to be discovered. In the NGC, an object classed as a globular cluster is NGC 6256. More recently the exact nature of this object has been uncertain, but it has been proposed that it is possibly a heavily reddened globular cluster at a distance of about 8 kpc; at present this object appears only in the catalogue of galactic globular clusters compiled by Kukarkin.

Finally, in this brief survey of professional catalogues, we come to the Catalogue of Star Clusters, Associations and Groups (Alter, et al, 1970) mention of which was made in Chapter 3. Here 12 objects are listed as uncertain open clusters, and all are to be found in the catalogues of galactic globular clusters of Arp, Alcaino and Kukarkin.

For the amateur, the percentage of galactic globular clusters which are observable out of those currently known is quite high. The number of globulars listed in Atlas Coeli is 100, and 60 of these are distributed north of the mean declination limit of this volume, $-30°$. In Chapter 3 mention was made of NGC 6558 and NGC 6642, both of which are globular clusters but have been included in the list of Coeli open clusters. Along with these two objects, there are a number of other omissions and an error in the Coeli globular clusters, and these are shown overleaf in Table 4.

Catalogues of Globular Clusters.

Table 4. Errors in Coeli Globular Clusters.

NGC 6256	Omitted.
6380	Omitted.
$17^h 45^m.7 \ -60°45'$	Peculiar galaxy partly obscured by a large patch of dust.
NGC 6558	Omitted; shown in Coeli open clusters.
IC 1276	Omitted.
NGC 6642	Omitted; shown in Coeli open clusters.
NGC 6684	Omitted.
NGC 6712	Omitted.
NGC 6717	Omitted.

Of the known globular clusters, there are 27 which are completely beyond visual observation with any telescope. These include the Palomar clusters and those objects detected in the infrared. Details of some of the latter can be found in Terzan, 1971, Astron. & Astrophys. 12, 477. A further publication of interest is Hogg, 1963 A Bibliography of Individual Globular Clusters, Univ. of Toronto Press.

8. OBSERVATION OF GLOBULAR CLUSTERS.

INTRODUCTION.

The number of globular clusters that can be observed visually in the Galaxy is considerably smaller than the number of open clusters. This is due to the fact that less of the former are known to exist; on the other hand a high percentage of the galactic globular clusters are observable with moderate aperture telescopes.

Differences are very apparent between open and globular clusters in the context of resolution. Admittedly many globulars will allow virtually full resolution to be obtained, but not all, and in many ways globulars can be said to be disappointing objects when they are compared with the varied morphology of open clusters. Nevertheless, attempts to resolve the more recalcitrant globulars are well worthwhile, and the fact that in many cases the observer is resolving stars at large distances will add interest to the procedure.

While observers situated in northern latitudes have no real equivalent of omega Cen available to their telescopes, they do have impressive clusters such as M5 and M13 within easy reach of their instruments. Furthermore, the 28 globular clusters in the Messier catalogue are all observable from the southern parts of the British Isles (some admittedly with difficulty) and these clusters furnish an excellent introduction to these objects.

For the remainder of this chapter we shall be concerned with cluster visibility and resolution in detail. In the process we shall cite a selection of observational results and discuss the problems involved by enlisting the aid of currently available data.

1. Intrinsic Factors.

Concentration Classes.

Details of Shapley's classification of globular clusters by the degree of concentration have been given in Chapter 5. In all cases the concentration class of a cluster will have a considerable bearing upon its visual appearance, and we have already seen that loosely-structured halo globulars at large distances are only detectable photographically.

The more concentrated a cluster is, the higher the surface brightness it will display, and it will consequently be observable visually at quite a large distance. The most distant cluster in Messier's catalogue is M75, at about 35 kpc, and the concentration class of I assigned to it aids in its visibility. For clusters of loose concentration, visual appearance and any resolution will depend upon their distances and to what extent they may be affected by galactic obscuration. Such clusters in the Messier catalogue which are easy to observe and resolve are all relatively close, such as M55 (Class XI) which is 4.6 kpc distant.

Observation of Globular Clusters.

Integrated Magnitudes.
In Chapter 4 we mentioned that magnitude figures for extended objects often bear little relation to their appearance at the eyepiece. In this field the structure of a globular cluster has an important function, as discussed above. However, no one parameter of any object can really be considered in isolation, and this is shown in the present section of this chapter, where, although we are dwelling upon magnitudes, we still do not stray far from the concentration classes of clusters.

We have seen that distant, low concentration clusters are visually unobservable, and this, it must be stressed, is totally irrespective of their integrated magnitudes, which are not particularly low. If we were to apply integrated magnitudes only as a criteria of visibility, then the cluster Palomar 5 $(V = 11.6)$ should present virtually identical visibility to an object like NGC 6426 $(V = 11.48)$. This is not the case, however, and the determining factors which make this so are the respective angular diameters and concentration classes plus, in the case of Palomar 5, the heavy star distribution in its neighbourhood. For Palomar 5 we have the following: concentration class XII; angular diameter 10'.3. For NGC 6426: concentration class IX; angular diameter 2'.2. It is easy to see from this that the large differences in angular size between these two objects is particularly crucial when it is allied to the respective concentration classes. Just how sparse in star distribution a class XII cluster can be is shown in Figure 10 at the conclusion of this chapter.

Brightest Star Magnitudes.
The most impressive globular cluster in the northern sky is M13, and in this object the apparent magnitudes of the brightest stars are about 12 mag. Not too dissimilar are the bright stars in M92, and, as with all globular clusters, these stars are red giants. It is only two or three magnitudes fainter than the brightest stars that we reach the RR Lyrae variables, so useful in deriving cluster distances. The magnitudes of cluster stars have, of course, a direct bearing upon the integrated magnitudes of clusters, and when related to concentration class have a determining effect upon the visual appearance of a cluster, whether any resolution is obtained or not.

For many clusters the mean apparent B magnitudes of the 25 brightest stars are available, and a wide range of figures are to be found. At the upper end of the scale the mean magnitude of the 25 brightest stars in M22 is $B = 13.03$; at the lower end of the scale we find $B = 17.51$ for NGC 7006. Although the brightest stars are therefore very faint in the latter object, its concentration class of I enables it to be seen in amateur telescopes, although it is not resolvable in the larger instruments, such as a $16\frac{1}{2}$-inch.

2. Non-Intrinsic Factors.

Galactic Obscuration.
Large numbers of dark nebulae are to be found plotted on the

Observation of Globular Clusters.

relevant charts of Atlas Coeli. These, however, are only the most obvious examples, and it must be realised that the actual distribution of obscuring material in the Galaxy is by no means as tidy and evenly-bordered as the Coeli charts would indicate. This is not intended to be a criticism of the way in which these dark nebulae are depicted, any other method would be equally impracticable, but it is necessary to state that obscuration is a patchy, irregular thing. For example, over large areas of the sky where Coeli shows no dark nebulae absorption is rife, and to obtain the true effects of it upon any object studies must be made of the immediate vicinity of that object. The reddening in the neighbourhoods of numbers of globular clusters has been obtained, and if we take just the Messier globulars in the Sco-Oph-Sgr regions we find absorption of between 0.12 mag for M70 and 2.38 mag for M14, which is a very reddened object, and not at all an easy cluster to resolve, even around the edges.

Cluster Distances.

The distances of globulars range from 2.7 kpc for a nearby object such as M22 to the very large figure of about 100 kpc for some of the remote Palomar clusters. From the point of view of the visual observer, distant clusters are within the light grasp of moderate telescopes only if their concentration classes are sufficiently high. The three great clusters seen from northern latitudes, M5, M13 and M92, all lie within an upper limit of about 7.4 kpc, and this, coupled with their high concentration and bright stars is the reason for their impressive appearance.

It is unfortunate that much nearer clusters than the above-mentioned three objects lie at too-low altitudes for their full effects to be appreciated by observers at mid-northern sites. Nevertheless, the wide dispersion in angular sizes and concentration classes of the northern sky clusters is more than adequate to cater for amateur telescopes.

3. Further Selected Clusters.

In the previous pages we have already introduced material which is relevant to this section, and our purpose is to expound upon this a little more. Therefore concentration classes, brightest star magnitudes, interstellar absorption and cluster distances will again feature. We shall also compare the distant cluster in Lynx, NGC 2419, with the Palomar halo clusters.

Many globular clusters which present difficulties in resolution are objects lying in the regions towards the galactic centre. For observers at mid-northern latitudes atmospheric absorption will add to any other problems encountered; observers in more southerly parts of the northern hemisphere will be less affected by the atmosphere when observing in the Sco-Opg-Sgr regions, but will not necessarily always achieve greatly superior results.

It is natural to expect that clusters which present difficulties

Observation of Globular Clusters.

to observers in northern Europe will not do so for observers sited
in more southerly latitudes of the northern hemisphere. In many
cases this is so, and clusters such as M4 will appear virtually the
equal of M5 or M13 when observed, for example, from the southern
parts of the United States. However, not all clusters will respond
to observations made from the latter parts of the world, even when
the larger amateur telescopes are utilised. For example, observation
made from southern California with a $16\frac{1}{2}$-inch reflector have failed
to achieve much resolution on certain clusters. Two of these are
NGC 6144 and NGC 6235; the respective magnitudes are V = 9.07 and
V = 10.23, and both clusters lie in regions where the absorption is
of the order of 1 magnitude. The mean magnitude of the 25 brightest
stars in NGC 6144 is B = 16.04, and in NGC 6235 is B = 16.56, and
this, regardless of the loose structure of these clusters (classes
XI and X respectively) explains the obtained results.

Two further clusters of interest are M69 and M70, both of class
V and separated by about 2 degrees in the sky. 8-inch observations
made from Britain have fully resolved M69 but only resolved the
outer parts of M70. M69 is the nearer of the two, and is more
affected by absorption, by almost a magnitude in fact. The lack of
full resolution shown by M70 must therefore be due to its greater
distance, which is over twice that of M69. This would have the effect
of reducing the size of the cluster, making the angular separation
of its stars smaller and the inner regions more compressed and hence
more difficult to resolve. It is of interest to note that although
these two clusters have a declination of -30°, which adversely
affected the observations, a 6-inch refractor in the southern part
of California produced identical results to the 8-inch refractor.

NGC 2419 and the Palomar Clusters.
It is not only clusters situated towards the galactic centre
which can show little or no resolution; others at higher galactic
latitudes can be just as difficult to resolve, often even more so,
in fact, and the prime factor in the context of visibility of such
clusters is their concentration class. We shall bypass clusters
such as NGC 6229 (z = +13.9; distance 21.6 kpc) itself not at all
a resolvable object, and take NGC 2419 (z = +25.9; distance 61 kpc)
as an object to compare with selected Palomar clusters.

NGC 2419 is often thought by many amateurs to be the most
distant globular cluster in the Galaxy. There are, however a few
with greater distances, including Palomar 3, Palomar 4 and the
cluster discovered in 1976, GCl 0422-213.

The term 'intergalactic tramp' has been applied to NGC 2419.
It is not a difficult object to observe with moderate telescopes,
its concentration class of II enabling it to be seen relatively
easily. The individual stars are not, however, resolvable, not
even the brightest ones, as they have a mean apparent magnitude
of B = 18.32. It is instructive to see how this cluster compares
with some of those other remote clusters discovered on the Palomar
Sky Survey plates.

Observation of Globular Clusters.

At the large distance of 61 kpc NGC 2419 can at least be seen with amateur telescopes, and this is due solely to its concentration class. The Arp/van den Bergh cluster (Palomar 14) is at the same distance, and shows the loose structure inherent in many of these objects. The integrated magnitudes of the Palomar clusters are almost 4 magnitudes fainter than NGC 2419. If, therefore, the concentration classes of some of the Palomar clusters were identical to that of NGC 2419, they would be within the light grasp of the larger amateur telescopes. Resolution would, however, still be impossible, as the brightest stars in the Palomar clusters (where known) are very faint, ranging from 17.5 mag for Palomar 4 to over 20 mag for others.

We have, in the space available, gone into the factors relating to observation of globular clusters at some length, and in the process dwelt much of the time upon objects for which resolution is either partial or totally impossible. Lack of resolution is not confined to too many clusters, however, many being resolvable right to the centre. Even some objects of loose structure in densely populated star fields being partially resolvable, M56, class X, and affected by over 1 magnitude of absorption, being typical.

As far as globular clusters in external galaxies are concerned, northern hemisphere observers have three clusters in the Fornax dwarf galaxy available, although from Britain at least they will present problems due to their low declination. Details of these can be found in the list of additional globular clusters, plus details of a not-too-faint globular cluster associated with one of the galaxies in the Virgo Cluster. For observers in the southern hemisphere there are many clusters in the Magellanic Clouds, but these lie outside the scope of this Handbook.

To a certain extent explanations of the results obtained by visual observations can be uncertain; observations of a given object by the same observer and telescope on two consecutive nights can produce considerably different results. Nonetheless, excursions into the subject are always of interest.

While globular clusters do not present the variety of form characteristic of open clusters, they are, nevertheless, objects of considerable interest, and the distribution of the brighter stars in fully resolvable clusters will often show structure that departs from the total images as depicted on photographs taken with large telescopes. Finally, to close, Figures 10 and 11 overleaf show the star distribution in the clusters Palomar 4 and the recently discovered cluster GCl 0422-213, depicting the great difference that exists between this type of cluster and objects such as M2 and M13.

Observation of Globular Clusters.

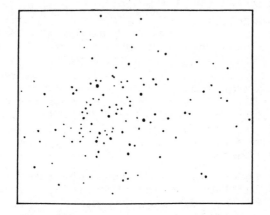

Figure 10. Star distribution in
the globular cluster Palomar 4.

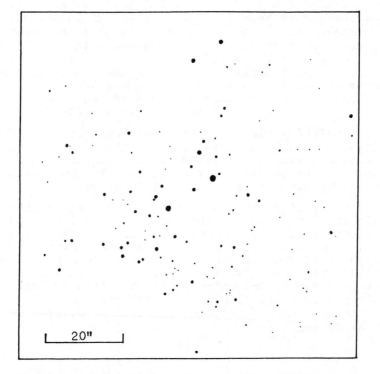

Figure 11. Brightest stars in the globular
cluster GCl 0422-213.

PART THREE : A CATALOGUE OF OPEN CLUSTERS.

INTRODUCTION.

The catalogue contains observations of 205 open clusters made by 12 observers using telescopes of 60 to 3-inches aperture and 15 x 80, 20 x 50, 10 x 50 and 7 x 35 binoculars. The observations are divided into two sections comprising a) descriptions and field drawings of 176 clusters and b) descriptions of a further 29 clusters for which no field drawings are available. Distribution of data within the catalogue is as follows.

The extreme left sides of the left-hand pages show the Webb Society catalogue number (WS), these continuing in numerical sequence from the last catalogue entry in Volume 2 of the series of Handbooks. Each Webb Society number is followed by the actual designation of the cluster while for those clusters which are Messier objects the Messier number will appear below the relevant NGC or IC number.

The remaining data, covering the greater parts of the left-hand pages, is as follows.

Upper Line.

(a) Positions for 1975.0

(b) Magnitudes of clusters.

(c) Angular diameters of clusters in arcminutes.

(d) Trumpler type of clusters.

(e) The abbreviated form of the relevant constellation.

> The data in (a) to (e) is taken from the Catalogue of Star Clusters, Associations and Groups (Alter et al, 1970).
> In a number of cases additional information will be found below the data displayed on the upper line of each entry.

Visual Observations.

The data below the dotted lines are, in many cases, contracted renderings of observations from the Webb Society files. The observations are set out in order of decreasing aperture, the figures in parenthesis, (12) (8½) etc., are the respective apertures in inches. All quoted magnitudes, diameters etc. are purely eye estimates. Where observations made by more than one person using identical telescopes are concerned, the results have been run together into a single section.

Field Drawings.

These will be found on the opposite pages to the relevant observations, and consequently number four to a page. All the drawings are shown in circles of 57 mm diameter, regardless of the actual field diameters in arcminutes. In some instances only the immediate area of a cluster is shown, and for these cases a scale in arcminutes is shown under the drawing. In a very few

A Catalogue of Open Clusters.

cases no scale is available.

List of Observers.

The following list gives the names of the observers whose work appears in the catalogue. Details are also shown regarding the telescopes used as well as the locations of these.

D.A. Allen	60-inch	Mount Wilson, U.S.A.
	20	Pasadena, "
	12	Cambridge, U.K.
	$10\frac{1}{2}$	Minneapolis, U.S.A.
	8 o.g.	Cambridge, U.K.
M.J. Thomson	$16\frac{1}{2}$	Santa Barbara, U.S.A.
D. Ambrosi	10	Regina, Canada.
S. Selleck	10, 8, 6 o.g.	Santa Barbara. U.S.A.
G. Hurst	10	Earls Barton, U.K.
S.J. Hynes	$8\frac{1}{2}$	Wistaston, U.K.
C. Nugent	$8\frac{1}{2}$	Upton, U.K.
E.S. Barker	$8\frac{1}{2}$	Herne Bay, U.K.
P. Brennan	8, 6	Regina, Canada.
K. Glyn Jones	8	Winkfield, U.K.
K. Sturdy	6	Helmsley, "
D. Branchett	3	Bishopstoke, "

Binoculars	
D.A. Allen	7 x 35
K. Glyn Jones	8 x 50
D. Branchett	15 x 80, 20 x 50

Observers and Accredited Clusters.

The following list shows all the open clusters that appear in the first section of the catalogue (with field drawings) plus the initials of the respective observers. Clusters are listed in catalogue order, i.e., in order of RA.

NGC	129	ESB, DAA, DB.	NGC	654	SH, PB, KS.
K	14	GH.		659	GH, PB, DB.
NGC	189	GH, PB, DB.		663	PB, DB.
Be	3	GH.		752	SJH, KGJ, DB.
NGC	188	DAA, KGJ, DB.		744	GH.
	225	GH, SS, DAA.		869]	DAA, ESB, KGJ.
K	16	GH.		884]	
NGC	381	GH, SS, DB.		957	SS, PB, DB.
	433	PB.	Tr	2	PB.
	436	SS, PB, DB.	NGC	1039	KGJ, DB.
	457	GH, DAA, KS, DB.		1027	SS, DAA, DB.
	559	PB.		1220	DAA, PB, DB.
	581	KGJ.		1245	SS, PB.
Tr	1	GH.	M	45	ESB, KGJ.

A Catalogue of Open Clusters.

NGC	1502	DAA, GH, ESB, DB.
	1513	DAA, KGJ, PB, DB.
	1528	GH, SJH, PB.
	1545	GH, DB.
	1582	PB, DB.
	1647	DAA, GH, DB.
	1664	GH, PB.
	1778	GH, PB, DB.
	1807	DAA, KS, DB.
	1817	DAA, GH, KGJ, KS.
	1857	GH.
	1893	DAA, GH.
	1907	GH, PB.
	1912	KGJ, KS.
	1981	GH, DB.
	1960	KGJ, DAA, KS.
	2099	KGJ, DAA, KS.
	2129	GH, PB, KS.
	2141	DAA, KS.
IC	2156	GH, KS.
NGC	2158	DAA, GH, PB, KS.
	2169	SJH, KGJ, KS.
	2168	DAA, KGJ, KS.
	2174	GH, PB.
	2194	DAA, KS.
	2192	DAA, PB.
	2204	PB.
	2215	DAA, PB, DB.
	2232	DAA, KS, DB.
	2244	DAA, GH, ESB, KS.
	2251	DAA, GH.
	2254	GH.
	2259	DAA, DAA, PB.
	2264	DAA, DAA, ESB.
	2266	PB, DB.
	2287	DAA, KGJ, KS.
	2286	PB, DB.
	2281	DAA, GH, KGJ.
	2301	KGJ, PB.
	2302	GH.
	2304	PB.
	2309	GH.
	2311	PB.
Rup	8	GH.
NGC	2323	DAA, KGJ, KS
	2324	PB.
	2335	DAA, PB.
Cr	466	GH.
NGC	2343	DAA, GH, KS.
	2345	DAA, PB.

NGC	2353	DAA, GH, PB.
	2355	DAA, SJH, DB.
	2360	DAA, KGJ, PB.
	2362	DAA, PB, KS, DB.
	2367	PB.
	2368	PB.
	2383	PB.
	2401	PB.
	2414	PB.
	2422	DAA, KGJ, SS.
	2423	DAA, PB.
M	71	DA, PB.
NGC	2432	PB.
	2439	DAA, DB.
	2437	DAA, KGJ, KS, DB.
	2447	DAA, KGJ.
	2453	DAA, GH.
H	16	GH.
	2467	GH.
H	18	
Tr	9	GH.
NGC	2506	DAA, KGJ.
	2509	DAA, PB.
	2527	DAA.
	2539	DAA, KGJ, PB.
	2548	DAA, KGJ.
	2632	KGJ, KS.
	2682	KGJ.
	6405	KGJ, DAA.
	6475	KGJ, DB.
	6494	DAA, KGJ, DB.
	6530	KGJ.
	6531	KGJ, DAA, DB.
	6568	KGJ, KS.
Tr	32	GH.
NGC	6603	KGJ.
	6611	KGJ.
	6613	KGJ, DB
	6633	ESB, KS.
IC	4725	DAA, KGJ, KS.
NGC	6645	PB.
	6649	PB, DAA.
	6664	DAA, PB, DB.
	6694	DAA, KGJ, KS.
	6704	PB.
	6705	DAA, KGJ, KS.
	6709	DAA, KS.
	6716	DAA, DB.
	6738	PB, DB.
	6756	PB.

A Catalogue of Open Clusters.

NGC	6793	GH.
	6800	DAA, PB, DB.
St	1	GH.
NGC	6811	DAA, GH, DB.
	6815	DAA, GH, DB.
	6819	DAA, GH, KS, DB.
	6823	DAA, PB, SS.
	6830	DAA, PB.
	6834	DAA, GH.
	6866	GH, SJH, KS.
	6871	GH, DAA.
IC	1311	GH.
NGC	6883	DAA, GH, SJH.
	6885	GH, DAA.
Rup	172	GH.
IC	4996	GH, SJH.
Cr	419	GH.
Dol	5	GH.
Cr	421	GH.
NGC	6910	GH, PB.
	6913	DAA, KGJ, KS.
	6939	MJT, SS, KGJ.
	6940	SJH, ESB, DAA.
Rup	173	GH.
	174	GH.

Rup	175	GH.
NGC	7063	GH, DAA.
	7082	SJH, KGJ.
	7086	KGJ.
	7092	KGJ, DB.
	7127	DAA, GH, KS.
	7128	DAA, SJH.
	7142	PB.
	7160	DAA, GH, DAA, KS.
	7209	DAA, ESB, KGJ, KS.
IC	1434	GH.
NGC	7235	DAA, SJH, KS.
	7243	DAA, ESB, DB.
	7245	DAA, SJH, ESB.
IC	1442	GH.
NGC	7261	DAA, SJH.
	7281	DAA, GH.
	7296	DAA, GH, SJH.
	7380	DAA, GH.
	7510	DAA, GH, KS.
Mark	50	GH.
NGC	7654	DAA, KGJ, DB.
	7788	GH, SJH, DB.
	7789	GH.
	7790	GH, SJH.

Below are shown the open clusters for which no drawings are available, and which form the second section of the catalogue. The format is identical with the preceding list.

NGC	103	DAA.
	133	GH, DAA.
	146	GH, DAA.
Mel	15	ESB, PB.
NGC	956	PB.
	1444	DAA, PB.
Hyades		ESB.
NGC	1624	PB.
	1746	DAA, GH, DAA.
	2112	PB.
	2126	DAA, PB.
	2186	DAA, KS.
	2192	SS, DAA, PB.
	2250	PB.
	2269	PB.

NGC	2331	DAA, PB.
	2374	DAA, KS.
	2421	DA.
Mel	72	DA.
NGC	2453	DAA, PB.
	2479	DAA, DA.
H	2	DAA.
NGC	6507	PB.
H	19	DAA.
NGC	6755	DAA, KS.
H	20	DAA.
NGC	7062	SS
	7226	PB.
	7762	MJT, PB.

A Catalogue of Open Clusters.

Part One : Descriptions and Field Drawings of 176 Open Clusters.

WS	Cat	NGC	Dec	m	AD	Type	Con
162	NGC 129	00 28.5	+60 05	10.0	11.0	IV 2 p	Cas

Nuc. of Cas OB4. Contains Cepheid DL Cas

- -

($8\frac{1}{2}$) Large group with possible sub-groups to the S; fainter members to the N and W.
(8) 20 stars x50; looks like two clusters (25' field)
(20 x 50) Very bright and large; easily resolvable into stars; aligned in a northerly direction.

| 163 | K 14 | 00 30.4 | +63 01 | - | 7.3 | III 2 p | Cas |

Contains about 40 stars from 10 to 14 mag.

- -

(10) Rich object in a rich field, appearing as a nebulous patch x40; well-compressed, including three doubles of 12 mag and below; requires HP to resolve; 29 stars in 10' x 6' area.

| 164 | NGC 189 | 00 37.3 | +60 55 | 11.1 | 3.7 | III 2 p | Cas |

Related to Cas OB4

- -

(10) Rather obscure and faint cluster of medium size; fairly rich with a few bright stars set against a background of stars of 12 mag and below.
(8) Roundish cluster about 4' diameter; moderately rich, containing about 25 stars, about 6 being of 10 to 11 mag and the rest much fainter.
(15 x 80) Bright, large group increasing in size with averted vision; scattered stars.

| 165 | Be 3 | 00 38.2 | +61 22 | - | 4.0 | IV 2 p | Cas |

Contains about 180 stars.

- -

(10) Glorious compressed cluster consisting of stars of 12 mag and below; hardly detectable at LP, and not fully resolved at HP, although superb at x400 in good seeing; 11.5 mag pair on the E edge.

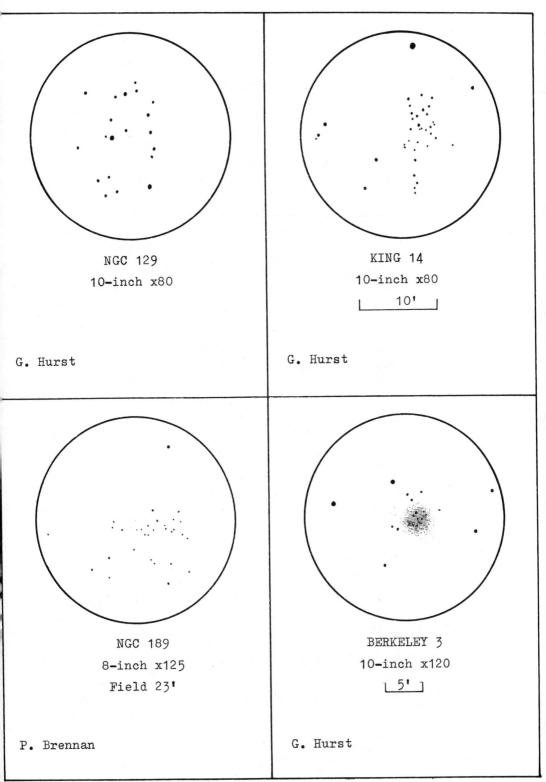

NGC 129
10-inch x80

G. Hurst

KING 14
10-inch x80
⌐ 10' ⌐

G. Hurst

NGC 189
8-inch x125
Field 23'

P. Brennan

BERKELEY 3
10-inch x120
⌐ 5' ⌐

G. Hurst

WS	Cat	RA	Dec	m	AD	Type	Con
166	NGC 188	00 41.9	+85 12	9.3	18.0	II 2 r	Cep

Contains stars from 10 to 18 mag.

- -

(8) Rather sparse cluster in which it is difficult
to determine the borders; a large number of very
faint stars form the background; can appear as a
rich group at LP; brighter stars to the south.
(15 x 80) Bright oval group.

| 167 | NGC 225 | 00 42.0 | +61 39 | - | 12.5 | III 1 p | Cas |

BD+61°154 (11.23 mag) on NW edge, is associated with
a small, bright diffuse nebula.

- -

(10) Loose group at HP; two doubles of 10 and 11 mag
stars mainly 9 to 11 mag; quite impressive at LP;
about 30 stars.
(10 x 80) Stands out well in rich field.

| 168 | K 16 | 00 42.1 | +64 03 | - | 4.0 | II 3 p | Cas |

- -

(10) A very compact, small, and possibly elongated
cluster; apart from 11 mag principal stars the
remainder very faint, although some 14 mag members
are visible x120; about 4' diam.

| 169 | NGC 381 | 01 06.8 | +61 27 | 9.4 | 7.0 | III 2 p | Cas |

Nuc. of Cas OB1

- -

(10) Considerable haze along a chain of stars; a
faint triple star just S of centre; aligned N-S.
(8) Up to 25 stars, 12 mag and fainter with a few
brighter members; about 6' diam.
(15 x 80) Very faint, compact group.

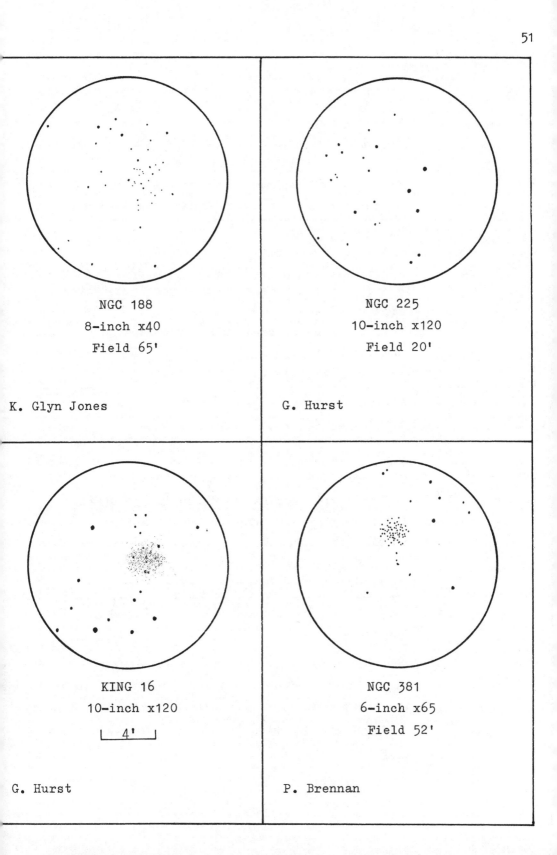

NGC 188
8-inch x40
Field 65'

K. Glyn Jones

NGC 225
10-inch x120
Field 20'

G. Hurst

KING 16
10-inch x120
|___4'___|

G. Hurst

NGC 381
6-inch x65
Field 52'

P. Brennan

52

WS	Cat	RA	Dec	m	AD	Type	Con
170	NGC 433	01 13.7	+60 00	–	3.4	III 2 p	Cas

(8) Easy but very coarse cluster consisting of two
long chains elongated almost N–S; the eastern of
these is the richer; contains one 10 mag, seven
11 mag and over fifteen 12 mag stars; 7' diam.

171	NGC 436	01 14.0	+58 41	9.8	5.0	I 3 m	Cas

(10) Fairly large, compressed group; stars between
9 and 12 mag plus a haze of unresolved members; x59
appears more dense on the p. end.
(6) Poor cluster containing about six faint stars
and others fainter; poor sight in a sparse field.
(15 x 80) Extends in a N–S direction.

172	NGC 457	01 17.5	+58 12	7.5	13.0	I 3 r	Cas

About 100 stars. ⏀ Cas not a member.

(10) Triangles of 9 mag stars grouped mainly to the
W; stars concentrated in small groups.
(8) 25 stars plus fainter ones in 25' field.
(6) Fine group of large and small stars; no sign of
nebulosity formed by unresolved members; 10' diam.
(10 x 50) Easily resolvable and very bright; stars
scattered and pointing in a northerly direction.

173	NGC 559	01 27.8	+63 11	7.5	10.5	II 2 m	Cas

Heavily reddened old cluster.

(8) Fairly rich group of faint stars in a wedge-shape;
elongated 5' x 2'.5 in PA 45° – 225° and widest at the
NW end; richest part precedes a 10 and 11 mag pair;
numerous faint stars, but not a first-rate object in
this aperture due to its faintness.

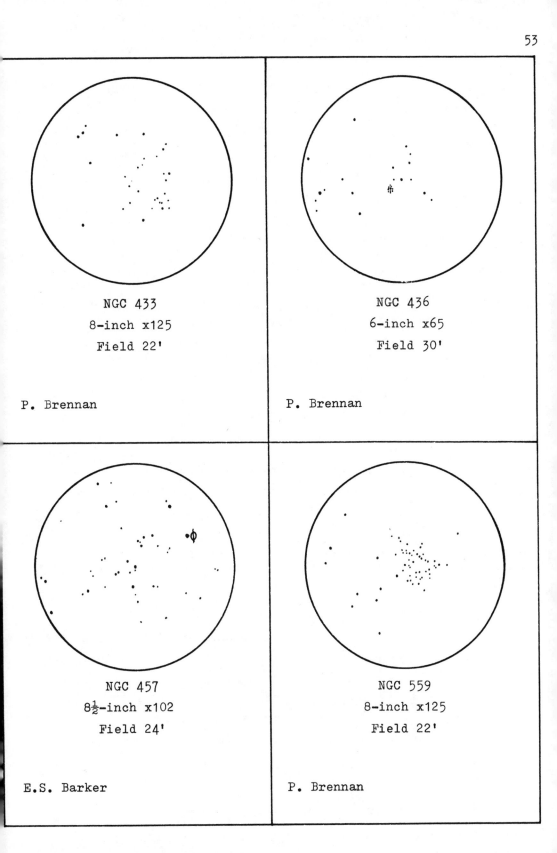

NGC 433
8-inch x125
Field 22'

P. Brennan

NGC 436
6-inch x65
Field 30'

P. Brennan

NGC 457
8½-inch x102
Field 24'

E.S. Barker

NGC 559
8-inch x125
Field 22'

P. Brennan

54

WS	Cat	RA	Dec	m	AD	Type	Con
174	NGC 581	01 31.6	+60 35	6.8	6.5	III 2 p	Cas
	M103	Brightest star 9.8 mag.					

----

(8) Not a very impressive cluster, being loose and
poor, and appears best at LP; contains about half a
dozen stars of mag 10 and about 25 stars of 11 to
12 mag; double star Σ 131 marked on chart opposite;
a red star lies near the mid-point of the NE side.

175	Tr 1	01 34.0	+61 09	8.8	4.0	I 3 p	Cas

----

(10) Two 10 mag stars and one 11 mag set against a
dense haze of unresolved stars; outer areas begin
to resolve at x120; 17 stars counted.

176	NGC 654	01 42.2	+61 46	9.5	5.0	II 3 m	Cas

Contains a number of infrared stars. Surrounding
interstellar matter has a mass of about 1500 $M_\odot$.

----

(10) Relatively loose group with rich part of
unresolved stars towards the N end; 17 stars.
(8) Coarse but quite rich in faint stars, particularly
the main portion of about 3' x 1'.5; ten 11 mag and
ten 12 mag stars plus many fainter ones.
(6) Small, nebulous cluster of 12 mag stars.

177	NGC 659	01 42.5	+60 35	9.8	5.0	III 1 p	Cas

Contains stars of 10 to 14 mag.

----

(10) Compact; haze of unresolved stars; close double
of 11 mag with a possible 3rd star involved; 10 stars.
(8) Faintest part to W; majority of stars are of 12
mag and below; 6 mag 44 Cas lies close S.p.
(15 x 80) Faint, rich large oval.

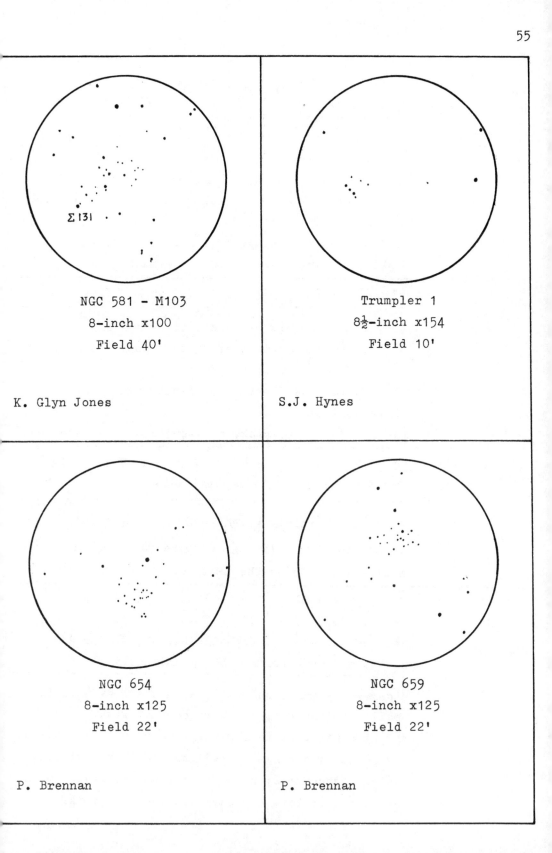

NGC 581 - M103
8-inch x100
Field 40'

K. Glyn Jones

Trumpler 1
8½-inch x154
Field 10'

S.J. Hynes

NGC 654
8-inch x125
Field 22'

P. Brennan

NGC 659
8-inch x125
Field 22'

P. Brennan

WS	Cat	RA	Dec	m	AD	Type	Con
178	NGC 663	01 44.3	+61 07	7.1	12.5	III 2 m	Cas

(8) Main body quite rich and two centrally situated parts very rich indeed, especially in faint stars; central region 8' to 10' and contains about six 10 mag stars including the close pair Σ 153, plus ten 11 mag stars and at least fifty 12 mag ones; a more or less roundish shape is formed by outliers.
(20 x 50) Large, very rich, irregular.

WS	Cat	RA	Dec	m	AD	Type	Con
179	NGC 752	01 56.3	+37 33	7.0	45.0	III 1 m	And

(8½) Irregular distribution; brightest members about 8 mag, the remainder averaging 10 mag; orange star on the S edge; about 50 stars.
(8) A very fine cluster containing many stars in pairs; fills a 65' field.
(10 x 50) Bright, rich, scattered; easily resolved.

WS	Cat	RA	Dec	m	AD	Type	Con
180	NGC 744	01 56.9	+55 21	8.6	7.0	IV 2 p	Per

Contains stars of 10 mag and below.

(10) Large, fairly bright and compact; about 35 stars from 10 to 13 mag; some pairs, these appearing most noticeable on the SE side.

WS	Cat	RA	Dec	m	AD	Type	Con
181	NGC 869	02 17.3	+57 02	4.1	30.0	I 3 r	Per
	NGC 884	02 20.7	+57 00	4.7	30.0	I 3 r	Per

Related to Per OB1. Cepheids UY, VY, VX Per and SZ Cas are members. NGC 884 is slightly older.

Observed by many, and a striking sight even in the smaller telescopes; 869 more compact with a very bright centre; up to 270 stars in both groups which have close groupings of red and blue stars at the respective centres; a red star lies halfway between the clusters; both are easy naked-eye objects.

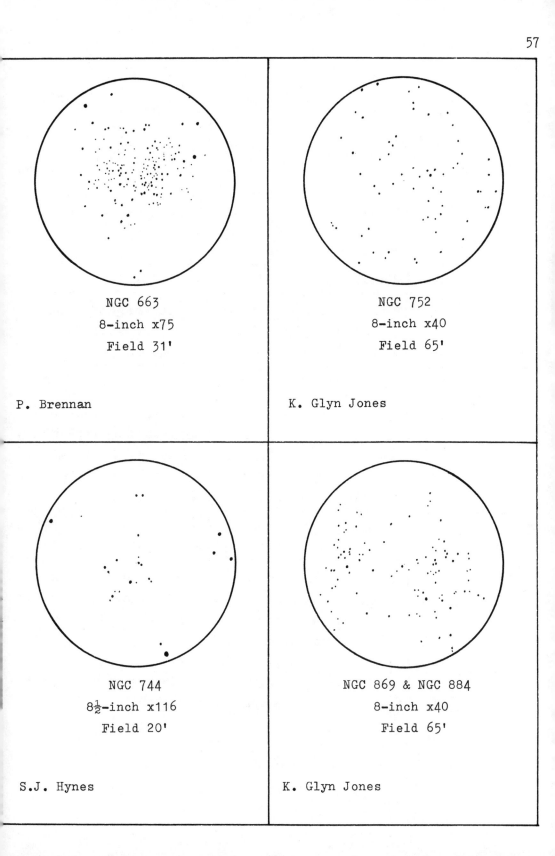

57

NGC 663
8-inch x75
Field 31'

P. Brennan

NGC 752
8-inch x40
Field 65'

K. Glyn Jones

NGC 744
8½-inch x116
Field 20'

S.J. Hynes

NGC 869 & NGC 884
8-inch x40
Field 65'

K. Glyn Jones

WS	Cat	RA	Dec	m	AD	Type	Con
182	NGC 957	02 31.8	+57 25	7.2	11.0	III 2 p	Per

(10) Pretty large, bright and compact; well-resolved
into stars of 11 to 13 mag with a haze of unresolved
members; about 44 stars at x44.
(6) Coarse group of faint stars elongated E-W; stars
evenly distributed in area about 10' x 4'.
(20 x 50) Faint, small elusive object.

| | Tr 2 | 02 35.3 | +55 52 | 6.9 | 20.0 | III 2 p | Per |

(6) x65 a bright, moderately rich clump of 9 mag and
fainter stars; main body about 15' x 5'; about 30 star
to 11 mag; some faint stars to the S.

| 184 | NGC 1039 | 02 40.4 | +42 40 | 6.0 | 30.0 | II 3 m | Per |
| | M34 | | | | | | |

(8) Large, bright cluster with three distinctive
curved arms of stars radiating from the centre; many
stars distributed in pairs, including OΣ 44 near the
cluster centre; naked-eye object in a good sky.
(10 x 50) Large, scattered; easily resolvable.

| 185 | NGC 1027 | 02 40.7 | +61 26 | 7.3 | 20.0 | III 2 p | Cas |

Regions of nebulosity lie in the cluster area.

(10) Large, loose cluster, very scattered in its
appearance; stars of about 11 to 12 mag with one star
a little brighter; x44 about 45 stars seen plus a haze
of unresolved members.
(8) 15 stars seen in a 15' area.
(20 x 50) Bright, rich and large; resolvable with the
stars scattered in irregular fashion.

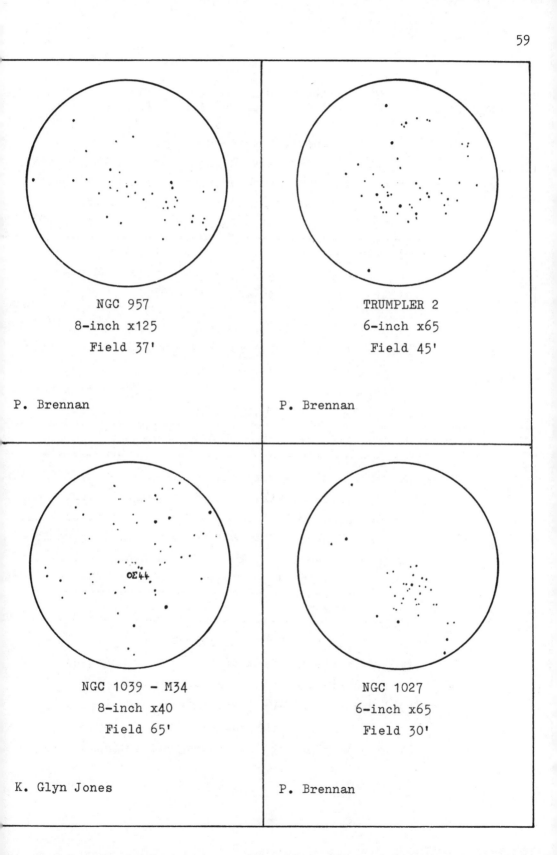

NGC 957
8-inch x125
Field 37'

P. Brennan

TRUMPLER 2
6-inch x65
Field 45'

P. Brennan

OΣ44

NGC 1039 - M34
8-inch x40
Field 65'

K. Glyn Jones

NGC 1027
6-inch x65
Field 30'

P. Brennan

WS	Cat	RA	Dec	m	AD	Type	Con
186	NGC 1220	03 09.8	+53 15	11.8	1.6	II 2 p	Per

(8) 10' diameter; unresolved.
(6) Small, faint cluster requiring averted vision; in superior transparency shows as a nebulous patch with a very few faint stars scattered across.
(15 x 80) Very faint, opaque haze.

| 187 | NGC 1245 | 03 12.9 | +47 09 | 9.0 | 10.0 | III 1 r | Per |

The Per moving cluster (Mel 20) is centred near this cluster at $03^h 20^m.3$ $+48° 31'$ (1975).

(10) x44 pretty large, compact, circular; stars of 12 mag and fainter; x148 resolved into about 100 stars but still appears rather hazy.
(6) Even distribution of 11 mag and fainter stars; x35 quite nebulous but resolved x65; 7' diam.

| 188 | Pleiades M45 | 03 48.6 | +24 01 | 1.5 | 82.5 | I 3 r | Tau |

Many observations were made of this cluster, for which a large field of view is preferable; excellent views were obtained with telescope finders and binoculars; a field of about 50 to 60', however, still reveals an impressive spectacle; the reflection nebula includes NGC 1435 and IC 349, and may be seen in small apertures

| 189 | NGC 1502 | 04 05.2 | +62 15 | 5.7 | 6.0 | II 3 p | Cam |

(12) 15 stars in 8' area; bright.
(10) Triangle of stars of fairly high magnitudes; is a well-defined object in a barren field.
(8½) Major axis E-W; 7 mag pair at centre; a very striking group at all powers.
(10 x 50) Bright object showing resolution.

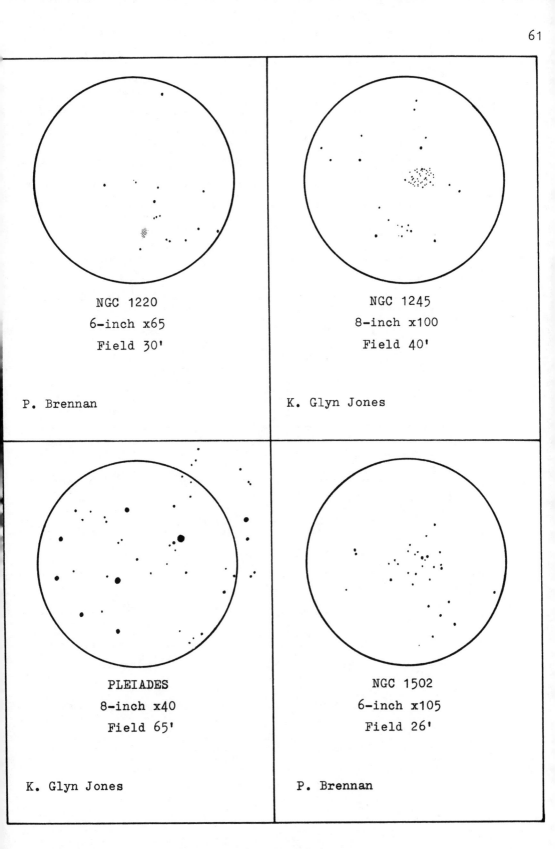

NGC 1220
6-inch x65
Field 30'

P. Brennan

NGC 1245
8-inch x100
Field 40'

K. Glyn Jones

PLEIADES
8-inch x40
Field 65'

K. Glyn Jones

NGC 1502
6-inch x105
Field 26'

P. Brennan

WS	Cat	RA	Dec	m	AD	Type	Con
190	NGC 1513	04 08.2	+49 27	9.0	9.0	II 1 m	Per

Possibly part of a triple group with NGC 1529 & 1545.

- -

(8) Poor object in a refractor, only 10 to 15 stars;
in reflectors at x40 small and faint with about 6
10 mag stars and some fainter; cluster elongated in
NW-SE line; about 8' x 6' diameter.

(20 x 50) Bright, fuzzy group.

WS	Cat	RA	Dec	m	AD	Type	Con
191	NGC 1528	04 13.5	+51 11	6.5	17.5	II 2 m	Per

About 80 stars are known members of this cluster.

- -

(10) Brightest members on the W edge; fine star
patterns with a group of 4 near the centre; about
50 stars seen in a 20' area.

(8½) Contains many faint stars in small groups.

(8) Moderately rich; about 42 stars at x80.

WS	Cat	RA	Dec	m	AD	Type	Con
192	NGC 1545	04 19.0	+50 12	7.6	15.0	II 2 p	Per

- -

(10) A triangle of one 8 mag and two 9 mag stars at
the cluster centre; a double of 9 and 11 mag lie on
the N edge; chains of faint stars trail from the
centre; 23 stars in a 12' area.

(15 x 80) Faint, large, rich object.

WS	Cat	RA	Dec	m	AD	Type	Con
193	NGC 1582	04 30.4	+43 48	7.3	30.0	IV 2 p	And

About 60 stars are known members of this cluster.

- -

(6) Contains about fifteen 11 mag stars in a 10'
area; a round, coarse, poor group surrounded by some
fairly bright stars.

(15 x 80) Bright, large and scattered; resolvable.

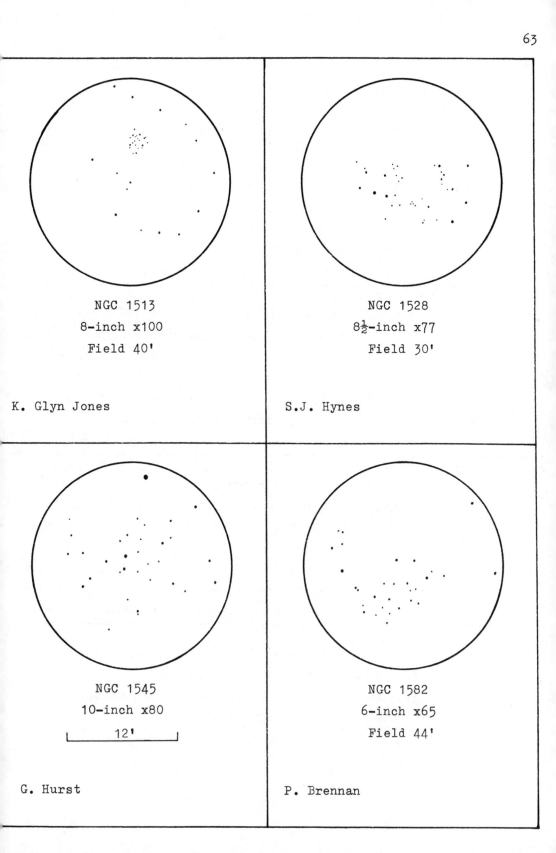

NGC 1513
8-inch x100
Field 40'

K. Glyn Jones

NGC 1528
8½-inch x77
Field 30'

S.J. Hynes

NGC 1545
10-inch x80
|____ 12' ____|

G. Hurst

NGC 1582
6-inch x65
Field 44'

P. Brennan

WS	Cat	RA	Dec	m	AD	Type	Con
194	NGC 1647	04 44.7	+19 02	6.1	35.0	II 2 m	Tau

This cluster is obscured by 1.17 magnitudes.

- -

(12) 60 stars seen in a 25' area at x80.

(10) Loose group spread over a LP field; rich in bright and faint doubles including a 9 mag with an 11 mag companion and a 12 mag pair in the N part; 53 stars seen at x80.

(20 x 50) Bright, rich, scattered object.

195	NGC 1664	04 49.2	+43 40	8.4	12.0	III 1 p	Aur

- -

(10) 7 mag star on the E edge; curving lines of stars run from the SSW to the NNE; rich centre with a haze of unresolved members; faint but striking; 41 stars.

(8) Many double and triple stars and faint chains.

(15 x 80) Bright, large, rich; resolvable except at the centre where the stars are tightly grouped.

196	NGC 1778	05 06.4	+37 01	8.3	6.0	III 2 p	Aur

- -

(10) Small group containing several doubles including an equal 10 mag pair at the centre; 20 stars seen at x120 in a 6' area.

(8) Situated in a rich field; about 20 stars of 11 mag and below; major axis aligned N-S.

(20 x 50) Bright and shows some resolution.

197	NGC 1807	05 09.2	+16 30	8.8	17.5	II 2 p	Tau

- -

(12) 15 stars in a 10' area at x80.

(6) Sparse group of 9 mag stars in a cruciform shape; several pairs of stars noted.

(15 x 80) Bright, rich, scattered cluster.

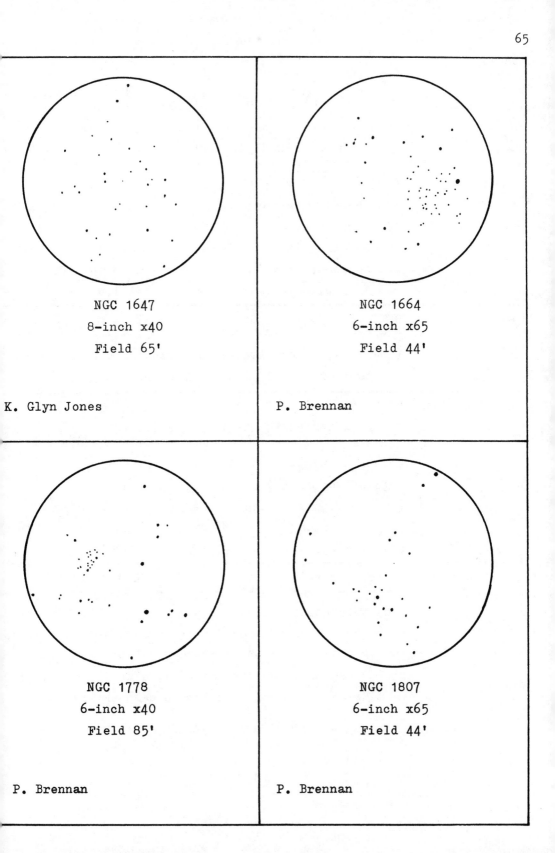

NGC 1647
8-inch x40
Field 65'

K. Glyn Jones

NGC 1664
6-inch x65
Field 44'

P. Brennan

NGC 1778
6-inch x40
Field 85'

P. Brennan

NGC 1807
6-inch x65
Field 44'

P. Brennan

WS	Cat	RA	Dec	m	AD	Type	Con
198	NGC 1817	05 10.6	+16 40	7.8	20.0	III 1 m	Tau

Possible member of a multiple group with NGC 1807, NGC 2244 and NGC 2252.

- -

(12) Faint at x80; 40 stars in 20' area.

(10) Regular in form and stellar magnitudes; at x77 18 stars seen.

(8) Requires large field; like two clusters with a gap between; many faint field stars to the NE.

(6) Rich with many 11 mag stars; 15' diameter.

199	NGC 1857	05 18.3	+39 20	8.2	7.0	II 2 m	Aur

- -

(10) 7 mag orange star at the cluster centre; rich in stars of 10 and 11 mag; 17 stars; diam. 7'.

200	NGC 1893	05 21.0	+33 22	7.7	12.0	II 2 m	Aur

The gaseous nebula IC 410 is associated.

- -

(12) x80 30 stars in 15' area, mostly around the edge of the field.

(10) Contained within a triangle of 8 mag stars; very rich with a haze of unresolved stars; 22 stars observed excluding the three 8 mag ones.

201	NGC 1907	05 26.4	+35 18	9.9	4.5	II 1 m	Aur

- -

(10) Nebulous at LP; two 9 mag stars on the SE edge; rich core of 12 mag and fainter stars; 16 stars seen.

(8) 12 to 15 stars of 11 mag and below; nebulous background of unresolved members; slightly extended in a NW-SE line, and lies in the same LP field as M38

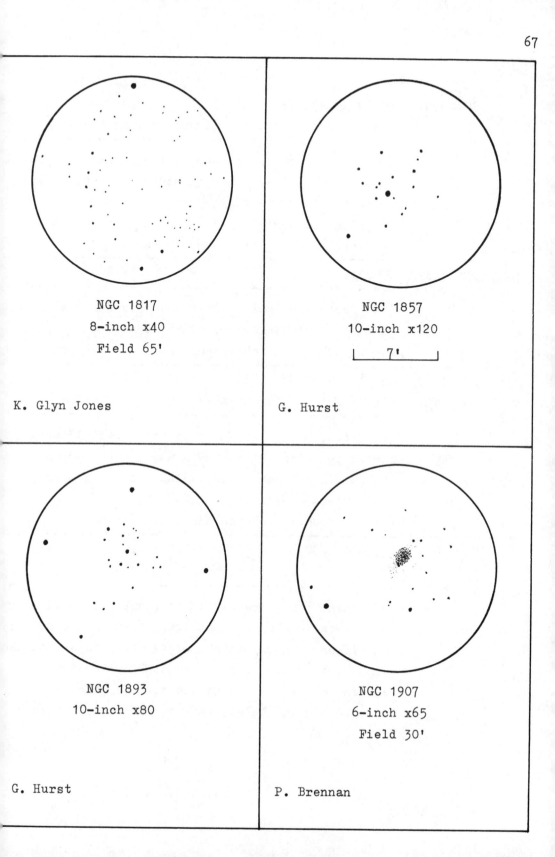

NGC 1817
8-inch x40
Field 65'

K. Glyn Jones

NGC 1857
10-inch x120
⌐─── 7' ───⌐

G. Hurst

NGC 1893
10-inch x80

G. Hurst

NGC 1907
6-inch x65
Field 30'

P. Brennan

WS	Cat	RA	Dec	m	AD	Type	Con
202	NGC 1912	05 27.0	+35 49	6.7	20.0	III 2 m	Aur
	M38						

The brightest star in this cluster is 9.7 mag.

- -

(8) Distinct cruciform shape, the longer arm of the cross in PA 065°-245°; a considerable concentration of faint stars lie at the cluster centre.

(6) Rich cluster; many 10 mag stars, pairs and a nebulous haze of unresolved stars.

WS	Cat	RA	Dec	m	AD	Type	Con
203	NGC 1981	05 23.0	-04 27	4.2	25.0	III 2 p	Ori

- -

(10) Several bright members and many faint stars of 12 mag on the W side; 20 stars seen.

(10 x 50) Large, scattered, resolvable object.

WS	Cat	RA	Dec	m	AD	Type	Con
204	NGC 1960	05 34.5	+34 07	6.1	15.0	II 3 m	Aur
	M36						

The brightest star in this cluster is 8.7 mag.

- -

(8) Loose, bright group containing about 35 bright stars; contains two curved arms; one extending to the SW; dense centre, including two close pairs, the most southerly being Σ 737.

(6) 20' diam.; contains many outliers.

WS	Cat	RA	Dec	m	AD	Type	Con
205	NGC 2099	05 50.7	+32 32	6.1	24.0	II 1 r	Aur
	M37						

Contains 170 stars brighter than 13 mag.

- -

(8) Contains hundreds of faint stars and a red star at the centre, which is the brightest in the group; the closest concentrations of faint stars are to the N and W; brightest portion about 20' diameter.

(6) Very condensed at the centre; the majority of stars 10 mag and below; haze of unresolved stars.

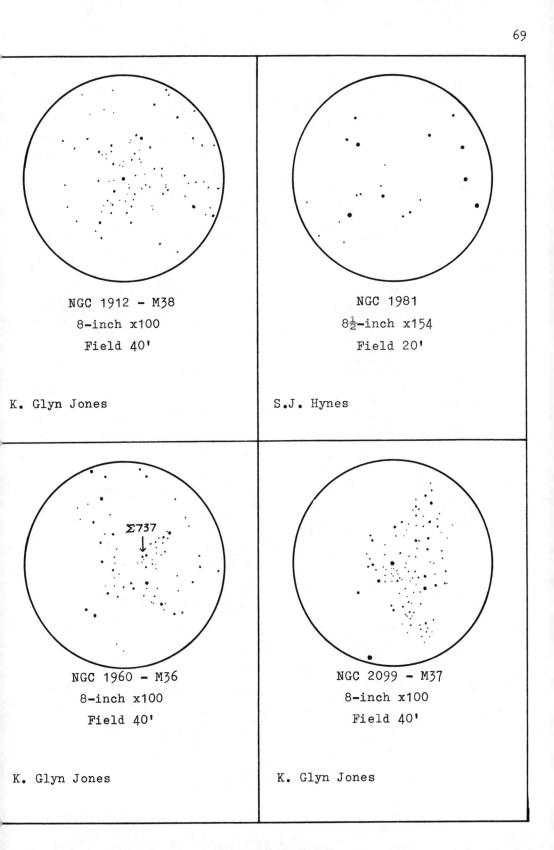

NGC 1912 - M38
8-inch x100
Field 40'

K. Glyn Jones

NGC 1981
8½-inch x154
Field 20'

S.J. Hynes

Σ737

NGC 1960 - M36
8-inch x100
Field 40'

K. Glyn Jones

NGC 2099 - M37
8-inch x100
Field 40'

K. Glyn Jones

WS	Cat	RA	Dec	m	AD	Type	Con
206	NGC 2129	05 59.6	+23 18	6.7	5.0	III 3 p	Gem

(10) Compact group with faint stars grouped around
a triangle of 8 and 9 mag ones; 17 stars.
(8) Irregular form; stars mainly of 11 mag and
fainter; stands out well at MP and HP.
(6) Nebulous cluster of small stars.

207	NGC 2141	06 01.7	+10 26	10.8	10.0	II 3 r	Ori

(12) At least 20 stars in 8'; not fully resolved.
(6) Nebulous and very faint; unresolved; 5' diam.

208	IC 2156	06 03.2	+24 12	8.5	5.0	III 2 p	Gem
	2157	06 03.3	+24 05				

(10) Both clusters in same field; bright stars are
lacking in both, and a background haze evident; a
9 mag slightly orange star on the S edge of 2157;
6 stars in 2156 and 9 stars in 2157.
(6) About 20 stars of 10 to 12 mag.

209	NGC 2158	06 05.8	+24 06	11.6	4.0	II 3 r	Gem

Brightest stars red giants, with absolute magnitudes
comparable to the brightest stars in globular cluster

(12) x80 irregular and barely resolved.
(10) On the SW edge of M35; hazy patch at LP; about
10 stars resolved x120.
(8) Faint, with a few faint stars seen; appears as a
small, nebulous patch at LP.
(6) Like cometary nebula at LP; at HP a curving form
of faint stars extending SW from a brighter star.

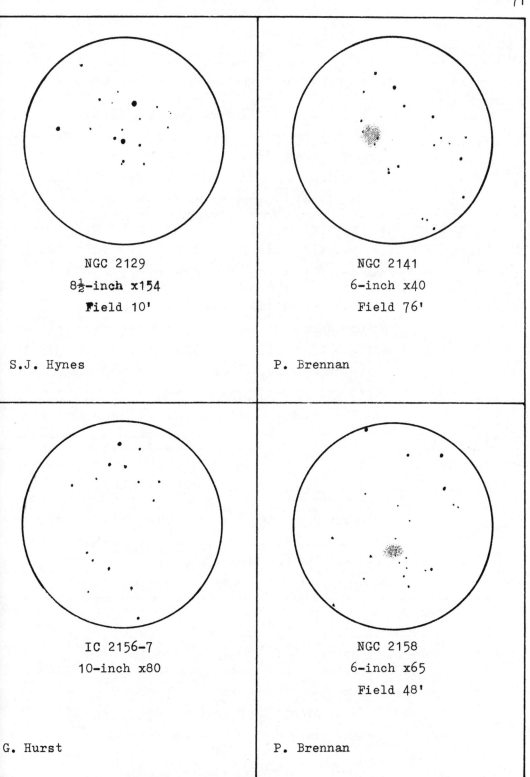

NGC 2129
8½-inch x154
Field 10'

S.J. Hynes

NGC 2141
6-inch x40
Field 76'

P. Brennan

IC 2156-7
10-inch x80

G. Hurst

NGC 2158
6-inch x65
Field 48'

P. Brennan

WS	Cat	RA	Dec	m	AD	Type	Con
210	NGC 2169	06 07.0	+13 58	6.4	4.5	I 3 p	Ori

This cluster is obscured by 0.17 magnitudes.

- -

(8½) 15 stars well distributed and showing a bluish tinge; the brightest star, of 8 mag, lies on the NE edge of the cluster.

(8) Reddish star in NW corner; about 8' diam.

(6) Small and sparse; stars from 10 to 12 mag.

211	NGC 2168	06 07.3	+24 21	6.0	29.0	III 2 m	Gem
	M35						

Contains 120 stars brighter than 13 mag. The brightest star is a B3 object of 7.5 mag.

- -

(12) Very rich; 110 stars in 25' area.

(8) Contains more than 20 8 to 9 mag stars, forming delicate loops and curls, with numerous fainter stars in the background; a curve to the NE ends in the bright star 5 Geminorum, (6 mag).

(6) Starless region at the centre; stars are mainly white, though one yellowish and one greenish seen.

212	NGC 2174	06 08.3	+20 20	6.8	15.0	IV 3 p	Ori
	2175						

Related to Gem OB1. Reflection nebula associated.

- -

(10) Just suspected x80 as a group of stars appearing out of focus; a small circular halo around a few stars comprises the northern part.

(8) Sparse; about 15 stars of around 10 mag.

213	NGC 2194	06 12.4	+12 50	10.3	4.0	II 1 r	Ori

- -

(14) Rich, concentrated group; brightest stars on the E part; many unresolved members show as nebulosity.

(12) 15 stars in 5' area; many unresolved members.

(6) Faint group, 6' diam.,composed of a number of 12 mag stars and unresolved nebulosity.

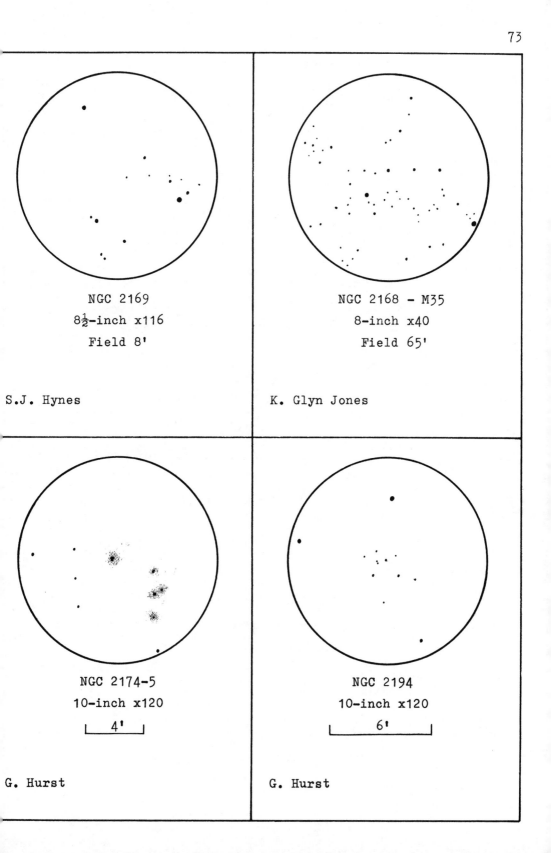

NGC 2169

8½-inch x116

Field 8'

S.J. Hynes

NGC 2168 - M35

8-inch x40

Field 65'

K. Glyn Jones

NGC 2174-5

10-inch x120

4'

G. Hurst

NGC 2194

10-inch x120

6'

G. Hurst

WS	Cat	RA	Dec	m	AD	Type	Con
214	NGC 2192	06 13.4	+39 52	10.9	6.0	III 1 p	Aur

(14) Faint group in a rich field; easy to pass over; no unresolved members.

(8) 20 faint stars in an amorphous group; 10' diam.

(6) Small, roundish, coarse cluster; about a dozen very faint stars across a nebulous background.

215	NGC 2204	06 14.6	-18 39	9.6	12.0	III 3 m	CMa

(8) Almost invisible at low magnifications, but quite easy at x125; the cluster is coarse, and contains 25 to 30 stars, some of 11 mag, but most 12 mag and fainter; main body 6' x 3', and with outliers this is increased to some 10'.

216	NGC 2215	06 19.6	-07 17	8.6	10.0	II 2 p	Mon

(12) 20 stars in 9' area.

(6) Small, coarse grouping of faint stars; contains about 20 to 25 stars of 10 to 11 mag and fainter; there are 2 or 3 stars brighter than 11 mag, but the cluster stands out well at x65; a 7 mag star precedes

(20 x 50) Large; tightly grouped towards the centre.

217	NGC 2232	06 25.5	-04 43	4.3	20.0	IV 3 p	Mon

(12) 15 stars in 20' x 10' field; bright.

(6) Sparse cluster around 10 Mon; 5 stars seen x60 and no increase x120.

(3) Bright, small, tightly grouped at the centre; easily resolvable.

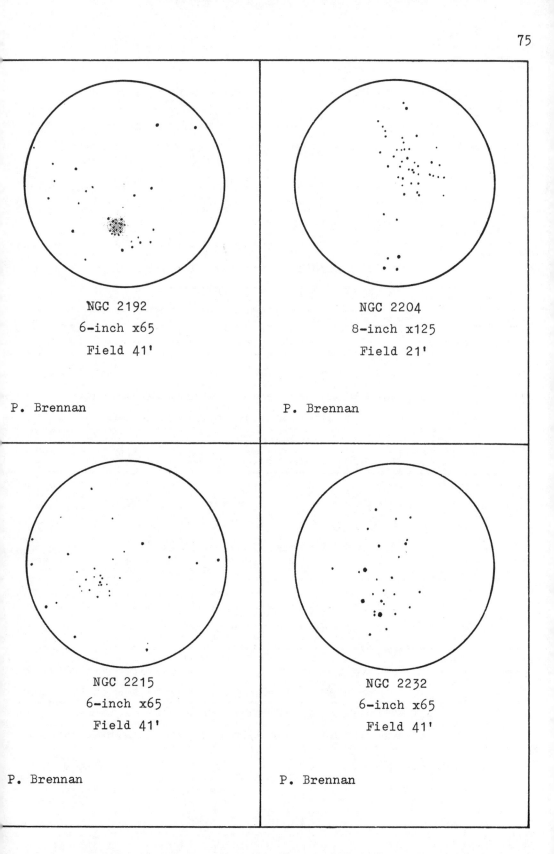

NGC 2192
6-inch x65
Field 41'

P. Brennan

NGC 2204
8-inch x125
Field 21'

P. Brennan

NGC 2215
6-inch x65
Field 41'

P. Brennan

NGC 2232
6-inch x65
Field 41'

P. Brennan

WS	Cat	RA	Dec	m	AD	Type	Con
218	NGC 2244	06 31.8	+04 53	5.3	20.0	II 3 p	Mon

Related to Mon OB1; connected with gaseous nebula
NGC 2237, 2238, 2239, 2246, the Rosette Nebula.

- -

(12) 30 stars in 20' area; nebulosity very evident.
(10) Large group dominated by 6 mag yellow star 12
Mon; 25 stars to mag 12.
(8½) Bluish and white stars barring 12 Mon; NW part
devoid of stars; very few doubles; slight indication
of nebulosity in certain areas.
(6) Very large cluster; no nebulosity seen.

219	NGC 2251	06 33.4	+08 23	8.4	8.5	III 2 p	Mon

- -

(12) x80 25 stars in a streak; 20' x 5' diameter.
(10) Elongated group extending NW-SE; chain of stars
stretching S contains considerable haze; 19 stars,
some reddish; in a rich region.
(20 x 50) Bright; centre parts brighter.

220	NGC 2254	06 34.7	+07 42	11.1	4.0	I 2 p	Mon

- -

(10) Very small, compact group forming a U-shape;
5 stars seen, of about 11 mag, these appearing in
a region of considerable haze at x120.

221	NGC 2259	06 37.2	+10 55	10.8	4.5	II 2 p	Mon

- -

(12) 10 stars in 5' area;
(8) x50 unresolved group 8' across.
(6) Very difficult, but glimpsed at times with avert
vision; a small elongation about 3' x 1' in extent
with some very faint stars scattered across it; a
faint star lies on the N edge; not seen at x35.

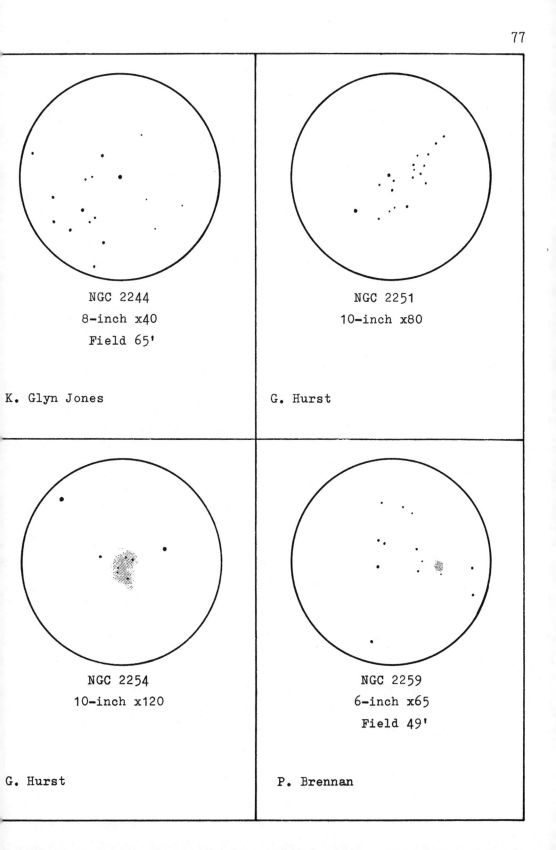

NGC 2244
8-inch x40
Field 65'

K. Glyn Jones

NGC 2251
10-inch x80

G. Hurst

NGC 2254
10-inch x120

G. Hurst

NGC 2259
6-inch x65
Field 49'

P. Brennan

WS	Cat	RA	Dec	m	AD	Type	Con
222	NGC 2264	06 39.8	+09 55	4.1	30.0	IV 3 p	Mon

Related to Mon OB1. This cluster is within an H II region with NGC 2259. H_2CO, OH and other molecules are to be found in the associated dark clouds.

- -

(60) The weak nebulosity just S of 15 Mon just seen in a rich field of bright stars.

(12) 40 stars in the 25' area around 15 Mon.

(8½) Extended almost parallel to the galactic plane; loose distribution; majority of stars 8 to 10 mag.

| 223 | NGC 2266 | 06 41.7 | +27 00 | 9.1 | 4.5 | II 2 m | Gem |

- -

(8) Outliers extend to 4', but the richest part is 2' in diameter; very rich in faint stars, plus a few 11 mags and a 9 mag on the S edge; about 35 stars at x205 and 20 12 and 13 mag stars in the centre.

(15 x 80) Oval; brighter towards the centre.

| 224 | NGC 2287 | 06 46.0 | -20 42 | 5.0 | 32.0 | II 3 m | CMa |
| | M41 | | | | | | |

Neutral hydrogen is distributed up to 1° around this cluster, which has a mass of about 600 $M_\odot$.

- -

(20) 55 stars in 15'; the brightest is orange.

(8) Roughly circular with irregular extensions, these mostly to the N; double star on the W edge.

(6) Contains many 9 to 11 mag stars, the predominant colours being white; at the centre 2 8 mag stars.

| 225 | NGC 2286 | 06 46.4 | -03 09 | 8.6 | 13.0 | IV 3 m | Mon |

- -

(8) Main body aligned NE-SW; a triangle of three 9 mag stars lies on the SE edge; 38 stars seen.

(20 x 50) Bright, rich and large.

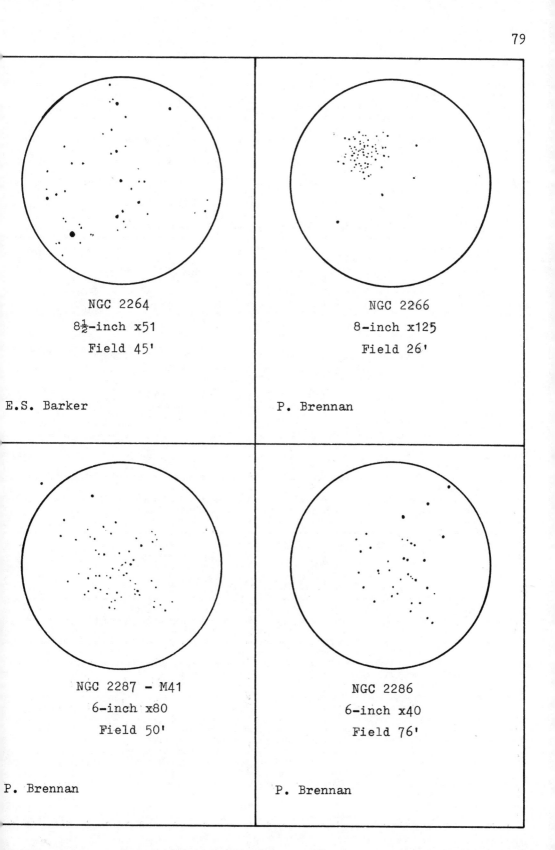

NGC 2264
8½-inch x51
Field 45'

E.S. Barker

NGC 2266
8-inch x125
Field 26'

P. Brennan

NGC 2287 - M41
6-inch x80
Field 50'

P. Brennan

NGC 2286
6-inch x40
Field 76'

P. Brennan

WS	Cat	RA	Dec	m	AD	Type	Con
226	NGC 2281	06 47.6	+41 05	6.7	10.0	I 2 p	Aur

(12) 30 bright stars in an 18' area.

(10) Two very close doubles at the centre; about 25 stars seen with fainter ones glimpsed.

(8) Very bright cluster with a kite-like shape; densest part less than 20' diameter.

227	NGC 2301	06 50.5	+00 30	6.4	15.5	I 3 m	Mon

Weak H II is visible on the Palomar Sky Survey.

(8) The major axis is aligned NE-SW, the S edge of the group being concave; contains 8 stars of mag 8 and 2 of 9 mag on the SW edge; a bright cluster with about 50 stars visible.

(10 x 50) Bright and resolvable.

228	NGC 2302	06 50.7	-07 02	-	2.5	II 2 p	Mon

(10) Neat, compact group, best seen at x80; there is a bright triangle of stars near the centre, plus some haze of unresolved members; a few faint double also noted; 13 stars.

229	NGC 2304	06 53.6	+18 03	11.5	3.0	II 1 p	Mon

(8) A very rich group of very faint stars, with onl a few being as bright as 11 mag; the cluster is abo 3' x 1' in size, being elongated SW-NE; the richest part forms the major axis; appears almost nebulous LP; averted vision advantageous.

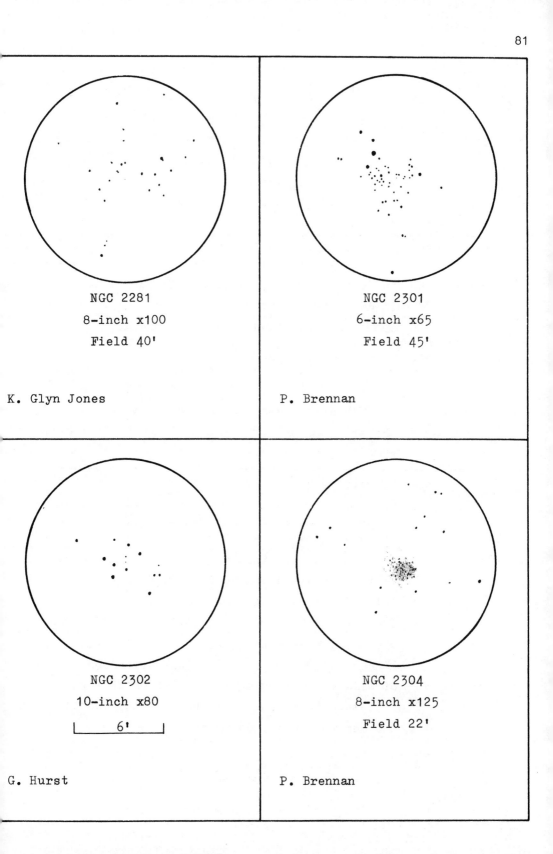

NGC 2281

8-inch x100

Field 40'

K. Glyn Jones

NGC 2301

6-inch x65

Field 45'

P. Brennan

NGC 2302

10-inch x80

|___ 6' ___|

G. Hurst

NGC 2304

8-inch x125

Field 22'

P. Brennan

WS	Cat	RA	Dec	m	AD	Type	Con
230	NGC 2309	06 54.8	−07 10	10.8	3.0	II 2 m	Mon

(10) A very small, rich cluster, with stars mainly
of 11 to 13 mag and below; contains much haze due
to unresolved members, and is not fully resolved
up to x120; a faint double lies at the centre;
3' diam; 9 stars.

231	NGC 2311	06 56.5	−04 33	9.8	4.5	III 2 p	Mon

(6) A fairly rich cluster of 11 mag stars about 5'
in diameter; about 20 stars seen on a slightly
nebulous background; in a rich field.

232	Rup 8	07 00.5	−13 33	−	4.0	IV 2 p	CMa

(10) Very faint, small and difficult; an 8 mag and
a 9 mag star lie at the N end; no other stars in
the area are brighter than 12 mag; 9 stars seen at
x80; diameter about 6'.

233	NGC 2323	07 01.8	−08 18	7.5	16.0	II 3 m	Mon
	M50						

This cluster contains stars of 9 mag and below,
many being reddened due to obscuration.

(12) 120 stars; circular centre, 8' in diameter,
from which stars spread in curved rays to give
total dimensions of about 25' x 10'.
(8) Appears as a bright, dense concentration in
the Milky Way; rich in groups of faint stars, and
stands out well owing to being surrounded by a ring
of slightly darker sky; red star on SE edge.
(6) Stars in a rough Y-shape; slightly nebulous in
the centre; in a rich region.

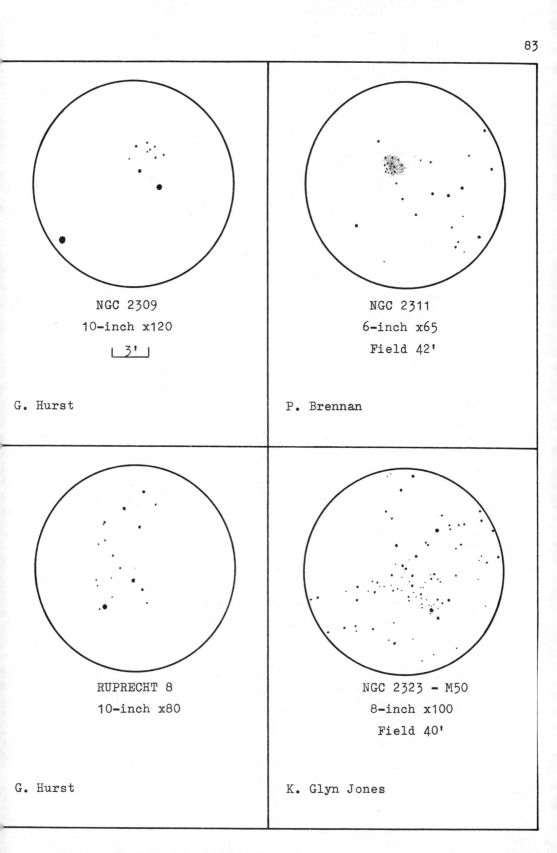

NGC 2309

10-inch x120

|___3'___|

G. Hurst

NGC 2311

6-inch x65

Field 42'

P. Brennan

RUPRECHT 8

10-inch x80

G. Hurst

NGC 2323 – M50

8-inch x100

Field 40'

K. Glyn Jones

WS	Cat	RA	Dec	m	AD	Type	Con
234	NGC 2324	07 02.9	+01 06	8.8	9.0	II 2 r	Mon

(6) Situated in a very rich field; in good seeing shows as a carpet of very faint stars, rich and quite compressed; roundish shape and about 7' or 8' diameter; two 9 or 10 mag stars superimposed, one central, the other on the NE edge.

235	NGC 2335	07 05.4	−10 02	9.5	10.0	III 3 m	Mon

Nuc. of CMa OB1. Possible double with NGC 2343.

(12) 20 stars in 15' area.
(8) Triangle of two 8 mag and one 9 mag on the SW edge; trapezium of 7 mag and 9 mag stars on the N edge; 11 mag stars at centre; about 30 stars.

236	Cr 466	07 06.2	−10 40	11.1	4.0	III 2 p	Mon

(10) Extremely difficult to locate and see; at LP it appears nebulous and at x120 a few stars are resolved, the remainder showing as a nebulous haze; no members brighter than 11 mag; diameter about 4'; 7 stars seen.

237	NGC 2343	07 07.1	−10 37	7.7	6.0	III 3 p	Mon

(12) 15 stars in a compact group 5' across.
(10) Intermediate richness cluster; a compact triangle of 9 mag stars enclosing a group of stars of 10 mag and below; diam. 7'; 16 stars.
(6) Triangular group; 3 bright stars and a few more fainter ones at x120.

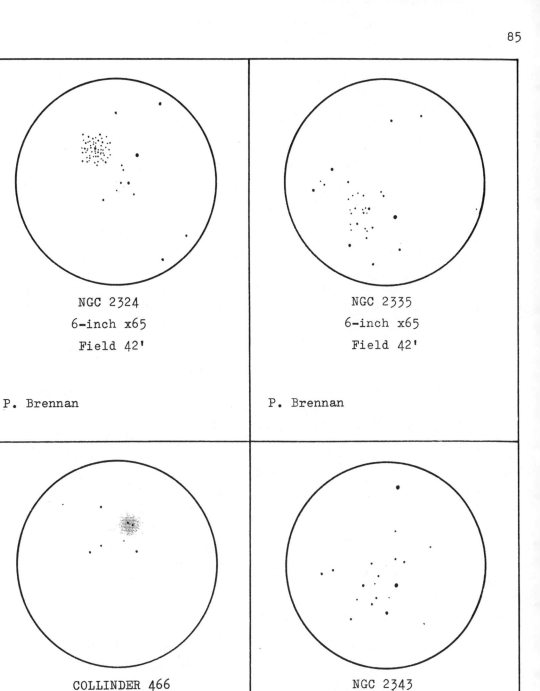

NGC 2324
6-inch x65
Field 42'

P. Brennan

NGC 2335
6-inch x65
Field 42'

P. Brennan

COLLINDER 466
10-inch x120
⌊ 4' ⌋

G. Hurst

NGC 2343
10-inch x120

G. Hurst

WS	Cat	RA	Dec	m	AD	Type	Con
238	NGC 2345	07 07.2	−13 00	8.3	12.0		CMa

(12) 12 stars in 10' area; more faint ones suspected.
(6) Fairly rich and easy; contains about 20 stars of
11 mag with 5 or 6 stars of 9 and 10 mag interspersed;
the cluster is much elongated NE-SW, and about 12'x 6'
in size.

WS	Cat	RA	Dec	m	AD	Type	Con
239	NGC 2353	07 13.5	−10 15	5.2	19.5	II 2 p	Mon

Related to CMa OB1.

(12) 35 stars spread over a 20' field.
(10) 6 mag star at the S edge with a 9 mag double
to the NE; about 30 stars.
(8) 7 mag stars at N and S of the cluster; curve of
stars from the W to the SW edge; about 60 stars
including probable field ones.

WS	Cat	RA	Dec	m	AD	Type	Con
240	NGC 2355	07 15.6	+13 49	9.7	9.0	II 2 p	Gem

(12) 20 stars in 6' area; very faint.
(10) Rich group, very compact around a 9 mag star;
11 mag double in the NW part; x120 needed to resolve
members; 22 stars; diameter 7'.
(15 x 80) Faint and very rich.

WS	Cat	RA	Dec	m	AD	Type	Con
241	NGC 2360	07 16.5	−15 36	9.1	13.5	II 2 m	CMa

(12) 50 stars in 15' area; impressive.
(8) Compact cluster; arrow-head shape pointing to
the E; 9 mag on E edge and 6 mag star to the W.
(6) Rich, compact group with nebulosity of unresolved
stars; tapering arm of faint stars and nebulosity
points to the S, ending with a brighter star.

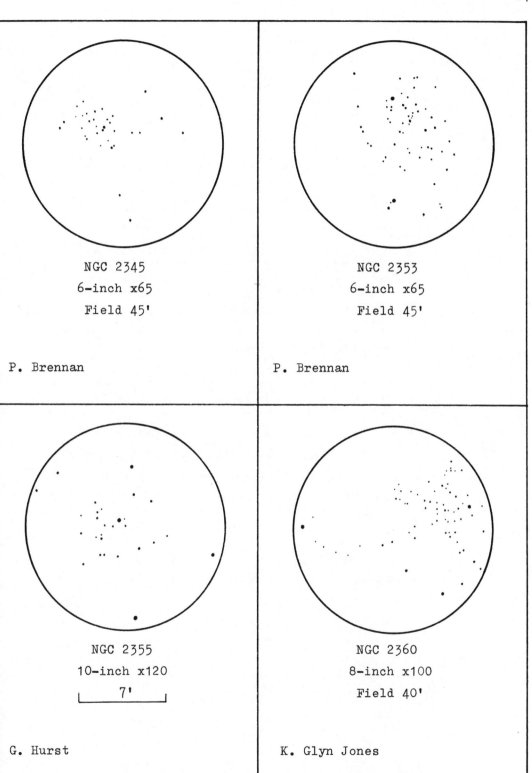

NGC 2345
6-inch x65
Field 45'

P. Brennan

NGC 2353
6-inch x65
Field 45'

P. Brennan

NGC 2355
10-inch x120
7'

G. Hurst

NGC 2360
8-inch x100
Field 40'

K. Glyn Jones

WS	Cat	RA	Dec	m	AD	Type	Con
242	NGC 2362	07 17.6	−24 55	3.9	16.0	I 3 p	CMa

Nuc. of Vel OB1; contains about 240 stars.

- -

(10½) 40 stars in 3' area plus outliers.

(8) 5 stars of 10 mag and 20 fainter members; the richest concentration surrounding and a little S of tau CMa.

(6) Not easily visible at LP due to tau CMa; 15 stars seen including the latter.

(3) Tightly grouped at the centre; resolvable.

| 243 | NGC 2367 | 07 19.1 | −21 53 | 7.8 | 3.5 | IV 3 p | CMa |

- -

(6) A small, coarse cluster; the 4 brightest stars, of 10 and 11 mag, are arranged in a Y-shape; the cluster contains about 10 members while fainter stars are evident.

| 244 | NGC 2368 | 07 19.8 | −10 20 | 11.8 | 5.0 | IV 2 p | Mon |

- -

(6) A small, roundish, faint cluster; contains about 10 very faint stars against a background that is slightly nebulous; an 11 mag star lies on the W edge; 3' diameter.

| 245 | NGC 2383 | 07 23.7 | −20 53 | 8.8 | 5.5 | I 3 m | CMa |

- -

(6) Small, faint cluster in a field of faint stars; it appears nebulous but is not a difficult object; the very rich field includes the asterism NGC 2384, shown on the chart opposite.

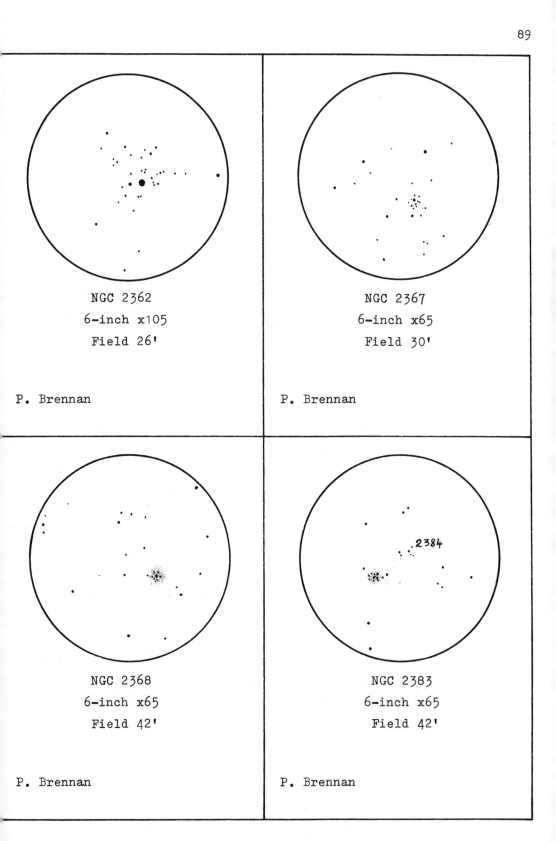

NGC 2362
6-inch x105
Field 26'

P. Brennan

NGC 2367
6-inch x65
Field 30'

P. Brennan

NGC 2368
6-inch x65
Field 42'

P. Brennan

2384

NGC 2383
6-inch x65
Field 42'

P. Brennan

WS	Cat	RA	Dec	m	AD	Type	Con
246	NGC 2401	07 28.3	−13 55	12.7	32.0	II 3 p	Pup

(6) A small, roundish cluster showing as nebulosity; shows very little central brightening, and is about 1' in diameter; situated among many field stars, it shows no resolution to this aperture.

| 247 | NGC 2414 | 07 32.1 | −15 23 | 7.8 | 3.0 | I 3 m | Pup |

This cluster is situated in outer spiral arm II of the Milky Way.

(6) A small cluster, 2' in extent, elongated W-E; it surrounds a 9 mag star, and with averted vision several very faint stars are seen; quite rich.

| 248 | NGC 2422 | 07 35.4 | −14 25 | 5.2 | 30.0 | III 2 m | Pup |
| | M47 | | | | | | |

The brightest star in this cluster is 5.7 mag

(12) 60 stars in 20' area; contains prominent double; (8) Contains relatively few bright stars; two arcs of 3 stars lie to the SW, and near the centre is Σ 1121, while Σ 1120 lies on the W edge; naked-eye object. (6) Loose; rich in bright stars.

| 249 | NGC 2423 | 07 36.0 | −13 48 | 7.2 | 19.0 | IV 2 m | Pup |

(12) 60 faint stars in 20' area.
(6) Contains a 9 mag star slightly W of the cluster centre; the remaining 40 stars are mostly 10 mag and fainter, and are quite rich and distributed evenly; some stars are in pairs and outliers extend to about 20', although the main body is 10' diam.; round, or just slightly elongated W-E; M47 lies just outside a 56' field to the S.

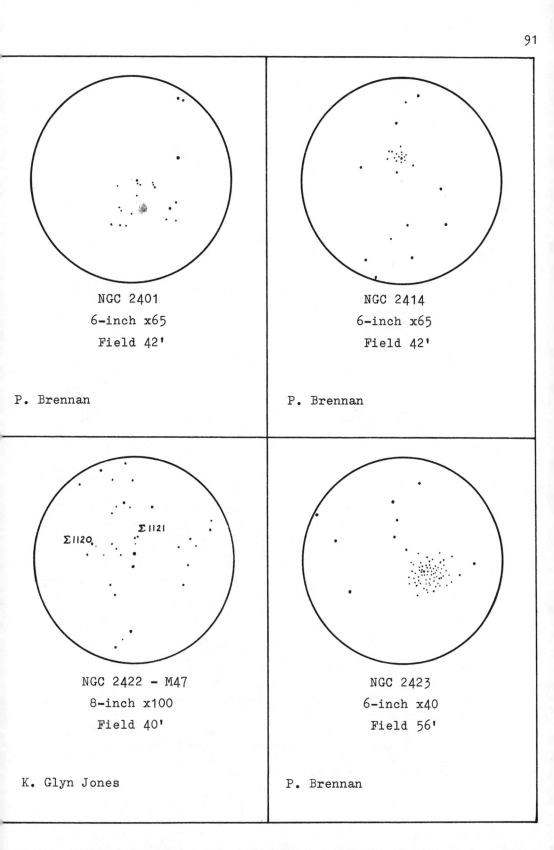

NGC 2401
6-inch x65
Field 42'

P. Brennan

NGC 2414
6-inch x65
Field 42'

P. Brennan

Σ1120   Σ1121

NGC 2422 - M47
8-inch x100
Field 40'

K. Glyn Jones

NGC 2423
6-inch x40
Field 56'

P. Brennan

WS	Cat	RA	Dec	m	AD	Type	Con
250	Mel 71	07 36.5	-11 53	9.0	7.0	II 1 m	Pup

(10) Round with great central condensation; like a
large, open globular cluster; about 8' diameter.
(8) 12 mag and fainter stars distributed across a
nebulous area; very compressed, and has a round
shape with irregular edges; 6' diameter.

251	NGC 2432	07 39.8	-19 02	10.2	4.5	II 1 p	Pup

(6) A small, very much elongated group which is
about 3' x 1' in extent; with averted vision it is
resolved into about a dozen 11 mag stars; somewhat
nebulous with direct vision; stands out well.

252	NGC 2439	07 40.0	-31 36	7.1	8.0	II 3 m	Pup

(10½) 15 stars in 4' area; other stars suspected.
(3) Bright, rich, with stars scattered in the outer
regions; easily resolvable.

253	NGC 2437 M46	07 40.6	-14 44	6.7	24.0	IV 2 m	Pup

Contains a number of extremely bright A0 stars; the
planetary nebula NGC 2438 lies on the NE edge.

(12) About 170 stars in a superb field of 23'.
(8) A fine sight; about 30' in diameter and very
rich in faint stars which are condensed in the
central area; the brighter stars stretch away to
the N and E, and there is a solitary 8 mag red
star about 20' to the SW; can be very faint in a
sky not completely dark or clear.
(6) Stars of 8 mag and below; some nebulosity of
unresolved stars following curves of the brighter
stars; NGC 2438 seen on the NE border.
(3) Rich and scattered; faint stars.

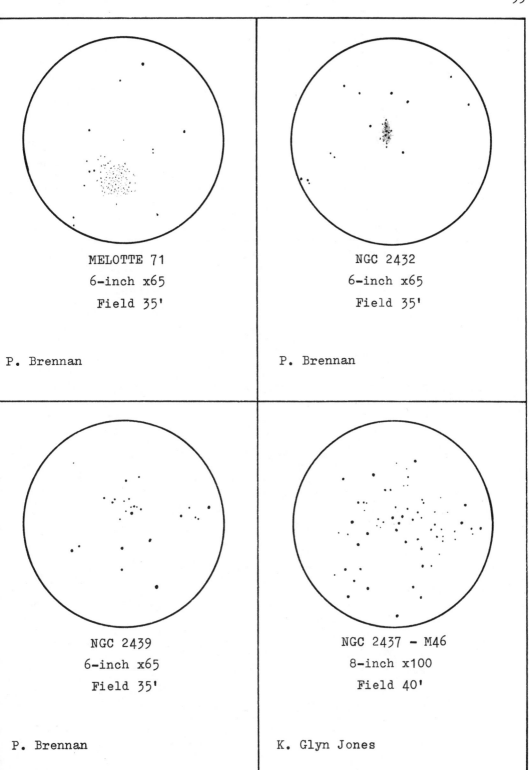

MELOTTE 71
6-inch x65
Field 35'

P. Brennan

NGC 2432
6-inch x65
Field 35'

P. Brennan

NGC 2439
6-inch x65
Field 35'

P. Brennan

NGC 2437 - M46
8-inch x100
Field 40'

K. Glyn Jones

WS	Cat	RA	Dec	m	AD	Type	Con
254	NGC 2447	07 43.5	−23 49	6.3	16.0	IV 1 p	Pup
	M93						

The brightest star in this cluster is 9.7 mag.

- -

(12) 45 stars in 12' area; faintish.

(8) A bright, fairly condensed cluster, containing
20 or more brightish stars and many fainter ones
concentrated towards the centre; the two brightest
stars are to the SW, and the brightest members are
spread out in straggling arms.

255	NGC 2453	07 46.7	−27 11	8.6	3.0	I 2 p	Pup

- -

(10½) 20 stars in 4' area; neat group.

(10) Grouped close to a 9 mag star; circular and
about 5' in diameter; inner condensed area in which
5 stars of 10 mag and below are seen.

(3) Faint and small; tightly grouped at the centre.

256	Ha 16	07 49.2	−25 23	−	2.0	I 1 p	Pup

- -

(10) Quite a severe test; apparent nebulosity NW of
a 9 mag star; about 2' x 1'.5 and possibly elongated
NE-SW; only 3 stars detected in the nebulosity; an
extension of nebulosity possibly seen to the SE.

257	NGC 2467	07 51.4	−26 20	7.2	12.0	imposs.	Pup
	Ha 18						

Related to Pup OB1. Ha 18b and Ha 19 associated. The
nebulosity is excited by HD 64315 (V = 9.23).

- -

(10) Apart from 2 stars of 8 mag members are of about
10 mag and below and scattered over a large area; a
nebulous patch just S of the cluster centre is Ha 18;
this is about 1'.5 diameter, and just S of a 10 mag
star; the only star visible in Ha 18 is an 11 mag
one just within the northern part.

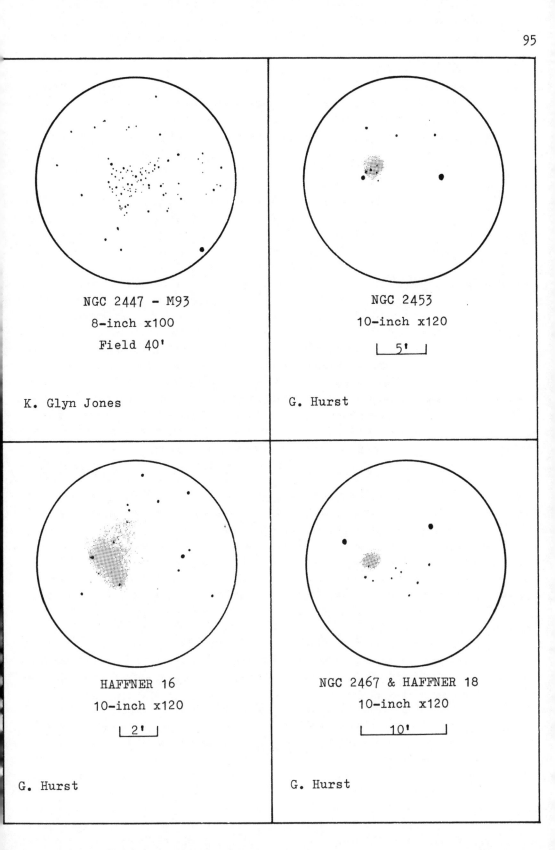

NGC 2447 - M93
8-inch x100
Field 40'

K. Glyn Jones

NGC 2453
10-inch x120
⌞ 5' ⌟

G. Hurst

HAFFNER 16
10-inch x120
⌞ 2' ⌟

G. Hurst

NGC 2467 & HAFFNER 18
10-inch x120
⌞ 10' ⌟

G. Hurst

WS	Cat	RA	Dec	m	AD	Type	Con
258	Tr 9	07 54.2	-25 52	9.0	6.0	I 2 p	Pup

(10) The cluster almost fills the field at x120; it
shows an irregular outline and initially appears
rather loose; at HP an inner scattering of faint
stars, the brightest being of about 10 mag, with a
heavily condensed region in the SE part in which 2
stars only are visible in nebulosity of 2' diameter.
15 stars seen in all.

WS	Cat	RA	Dec	m	AD	Type	Con
259	NGC 2506	07 58.9	-10 43	8.3	10.0	I 2 r	Mon

(12) 15 stars barely resolved, others not resolved.
(8) Faint, dusty cluster, about 10' diameter, with
8 to 10 stars of 10 mag and many fainter; not very
impressive

WS	Cat	RA	Dec	m	AD	Type	Con
260	NGC 2509	07 59.6	-19 00	9.3	5.0	II 1 p	Pup

(12) 10 stars only seen, and others suspected.
(6) Faint, roundish, nebulous object with a brighter
centre; well-resolved at the edges and to a lesser
extent in the middle; the cluster stars are very
faint, but stand out well in a rich field; 5' diam.

WS	Cat	RA	Dec	m	AD	Type	Con
261	NGC 2527	08 04.2	-28 05	8.0	22.5	III 1 p	Pup

(10½) x140 60 stars in 7' x 4' group.
(6) A moderately rich but coarse cluster, some
20' x 15' in extent and elongated E-W; the brightest
members of 9 and 10 mag lie near the E edge; about
half the members are fainter than 11 mag; a line of
3 mag 8 and mag 9 stars, 8' long lie 15' SE, and aid
in identification.

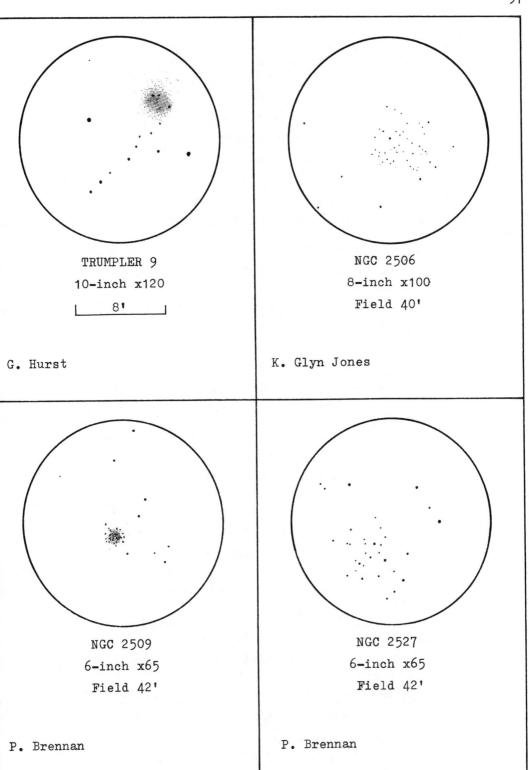

TRUMPLER 9
10-inch x120
└─── 8' ───┘

G. Hurst

NGC 2506
8-inch x100
Field 40'

K. Glyn Jones

NGC 2509
6-inch x65
Field 42'

P. Brennan

NGC 2527
6-inch x65
Field 42'

P. Brennan

WS	Cat	RA	Dec	m	AD	Type	Con
262	NGC 2539	08 09.6	-12 45	7.9	20.5	II 1 m	Pup

19 Pup (4.5 mag) lies close to the E.

- -

(12) 60 stars in 12' area.

(8) Large, very numerous but faint; dark background.

(6) Outline irregular and more or less triangular;
contains many little clumps and pairs of stars, is
quite rich overall and very rich in places; about
75 stars, mostly of 11 and 12 mag; about 20' diam.

263	NGC 2548	08 12.4	-05 43	5.2	30.0	I 2 m	Hya
	M48						

Contains 50 stars to 13 mag.

- -

(12) 70 stars in 25' area; central group shaped like
an elongated letter S.

(8) Forms a distinct, almost equilateral triangle;
many of the fainter stars are grouped in small pairs
the surrounding sky is quite dark, and the cluster i
quite self-contained; naked-eye object in a good sky

264	NGC 2632	08 38.6	+20 05	5.2	90.0	II 2 m	Cnc
	M44						

Contains over 2000 stars. Doubles are numerous. The
variable S Cnc (8 - 10 mag: 9.48d) appears within th
cluster stars but is not a member.

- -

In anything but a rich-field telescope this cluster
is generally too large for the field of view; the
brighter stars have a yellowish hue, and one observe
records a 9 mag greenish star near the centre; it is
an easy naked-eye object.

265	NGC 2682	08 49.2	+11 54	7.5	14.5	II 2 m	Cnc
	M67						

Contains about 500 stars from 10 to 16 mag.

- -

(8) Bright object in a fairly dark part of the sky;
brightest star is on the NE edge and about 8 mag; in
the central area there are about 20 stars of 10 to
12 mag; more than 60 stars within a 7'.5 radius.

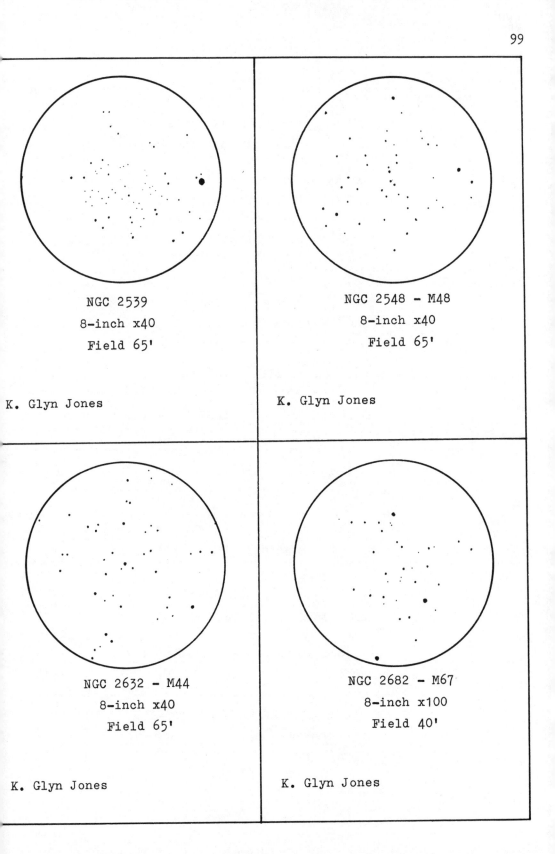

NGC 2539
8-inch x40
Field 65'

K. Glyn Jones

NGC 2548 - M48
8-inch x40
Field 65'

K. Glyn Jones

NGC 2632 - M44
8-inch x40
Field 65'

K. Glyn Jones

NGC 2682 - M67
8-inch x100
Field 40'

K. Glyn Jones

WS	Cat	RA	Dec	m	AD	Type	Con
266	NGC 6405	17 38.4	−32 12	5.3	26.0	III 2 p	Sco
	M6						

The second brightest star is HD 160202, a flare star which showed a 5 mag increase in 40 min in 1965.

- -

(8) Rich, brilliant cluster containing groups of small, faint stars among very many bright ones; not easily seen from latitudes higher than 50° N.
(7 x 35) Large, beautiful cluster, well seen.

WS	Cat	RA	Dec	m	AD	Type	Con
267	NGC 6475	17 52.3	−34 48	4.1	50.0	II 2 r	Sco
	M7						

- -

A large cluster best observed through the finder telescope; a bright, fairly close pair is at the centre with a yellow star SW of centre; a 3-inch will also give good results on this object.

WS	Cat	RA	Dec	m	AD	Type	Con
268	NGC 6494	17 55.5	−19 01	6.9	27.0	III 1 m	Sgr
	M23						

Contains about 120 stars of 10 mag and below.

- -

(12) 100 stars in a 22' field.
(8) Fine, bright cluster of 10 to 13 mag stars; a 6 mag star is close to the NW, and the group shows a fan-like shape spreading from an 8 mag star to the NE; main parts fit into a 40' field.
(10 x 50) Large and bright; easily resolvable.

WS	Cat	RA	Dec	m	AD	Type	Con
269	NGC 6530	18 01.7	−24 23	6.3	5.0	I 2 m	Sgr
	M8						

Cluster associated with NGC 6523, an emission nebula described in Volume 2.

- -

In binoculars or small telescopes the cluster can be seen to appear slightly nebulous; the cluster is not very rich or impressive, but is sufficiently bright to be seen with the naked eye from Great Britain and the northern U.S.A.

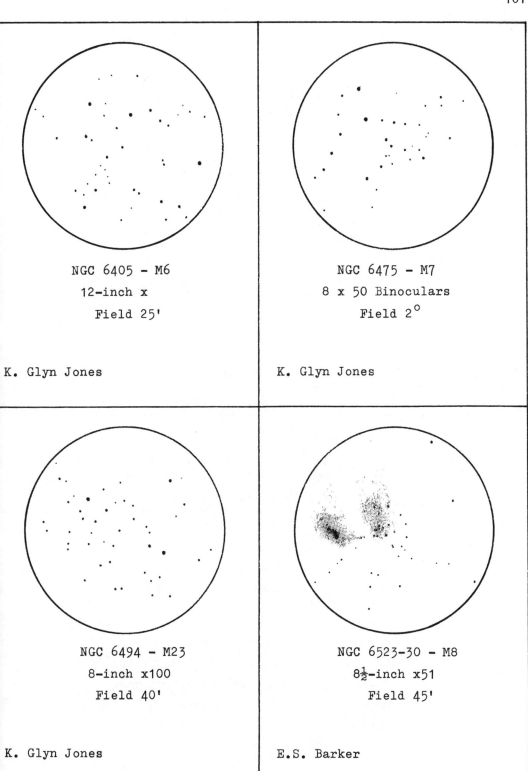

NGC 6405 - M6
12-inch x
Field 25'

K. Glyn Jones

NGC 6475 - M7
8 x 50 Binoculars
Field 2°

K. Glyn Jones

NGC 6494 - M23
8-inch x100
Field 40'

K. Glyn Jones

NGC 6523-30 - M8
8½-inch x51
Field 45'

E.S. Barker

WS	Cat	RA	Dec	m	AD	Type	Con
270	NGC 6531	18 03.1	−22 30	6.7	12.0	I 3 m	Sgr
	M21						

Contains about 60 stars of 8 mag and below; large clouds of obscuring dust surround the cluster.

- -

(8) A smallish. fairly compact cluster at the NE of a double string of fairly bright stars which connect it with the nebula M20; rather sparse and formless, about 20 stars being visible.

(3) Bright and easily resolvable.

271	NGC 6568	18 11.3	−21 36	8.4	13.0	III 1 m	Sgr

(8) Rather faint and open with few bright stars; an S-shaped curve in the centre surrounded by a fine dusting of faint members; 14 Sgr (5.5 mag) lies 20' to the E.

(6) Sparse, with slightly nebulous centre; 23 stars.

272	Tr 32	18 16.1	−13 21	12.2	4.0	I 2 m	Ser

(10) Very faint, small and difficult; the brightest star is of 12 mag, and x120 needed to resolve the few members shown; evidence of a very rich object requiring a large aperture; about 3' diameter.

273	NGC 6603	18 17.0	−18 25	11.8	5.0	I 1 r	Sgr
	[M24]						

This cluster is situated in a star-cloud, the latter being the object catalogued by Messier. The cloud is about 1.5° in diameter and of 4.6 mag.

- -

(8) NGC 6603 lies to the NE of M24 directly N of a red or orange star; seems nebulous due to its faintness; at HP, in good conditions, it shows as a dense cluster containing several narrow, curved dark lanes; M24 is an easy naked-eye object, and a good view can be obtained by binoculars.

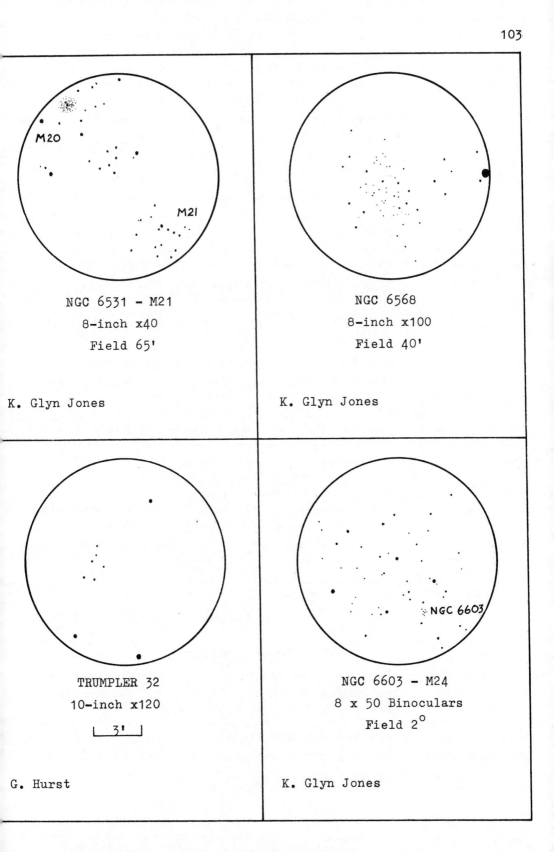

M20

M21

NGC 6531 - M21
8-inch x40
Field 65'

K. Glyn Jones

NGC 6568
8-inch x100
Field 40'

K. Glyn Jones

TRUMPLER 32
10-inch x120
3'

G. Hurst

NGC 6603

NGC 6603 - M24
8 x 50 Binoculars
Field 2°

K. Glyn Jones

WS	Cat	RA	Dec	m	AD	Type	Con
274	NGC 6611	18 17.4	−13 47	6.4	8.0	II 3 m	Ser
	M16						

Contains a large number of faint, red stars, these
possibly reddened due to obscuration.

- -

(8) Situated at the N end of a large, curving 'S'
of bright stars; a fine, conspicuous cluster with
nebulosity associated, details of which are to be
found in Volume 2.

275	NGC 6613	18 18.5	−17 08	8.5	7.0	II 3 p	Sgr
	M18						

This cluster is obscured by 1.4 magnitudes.

- -

(8) Rather an inconspicuous cluster with one or two
brightish stars and the remaining fainter ones
forming something of an 'S' shape; rather difficult
to pick out from many other groups in the region.
(15 x 80) Appears rich and more compressed.

276	NGC 6633	18 26.3	+06 33	6.0	25.0	III 2 m	Oph

(12) 35 stars in a 20' field.
(8½) Large, loose cluster with the majority of stars
of 8 to 10 mag; a small, arrow-shaped group lies on
the NW edge; a fine LP field.
(6) The brighter stars W-shaped; a magnificent group
easily visible to the naked eye.

277	IC 4725	18 30.3	−19 16	6.5	35.0	I 2 p	Sgr
	M25						

Contains the Cepheid U Sgr, discovered in 1956.

- -

(12) 40 stars in20' field; compact centre.
(8) A fine, though rather open group with a dark
background; a bright, slightly yellow star lies near
the centre; can be a little difficult to separate
from other nearby fields.
(6) About 22' x 15' diameter; stars of 7 mag and
below, including one red; fine group.

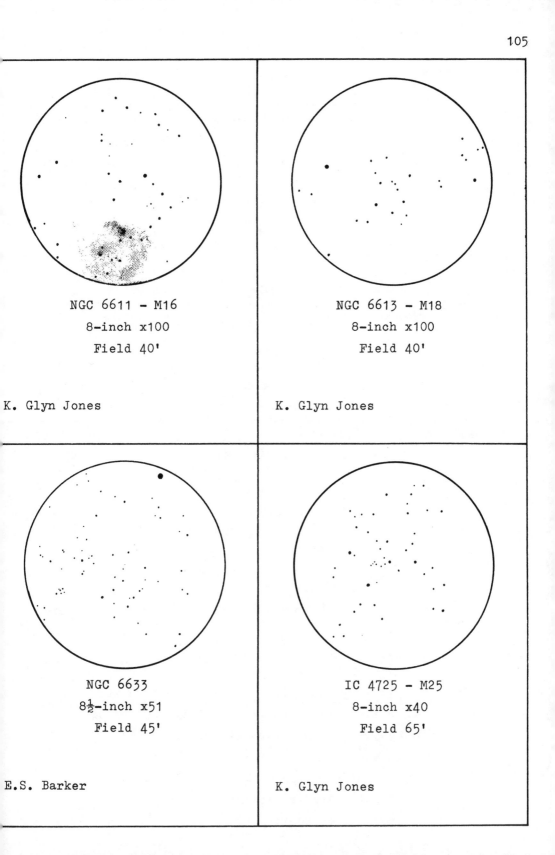

NGC 6611 - M16
8-inch x100
Field 40'

K. Glyn Jones

NGC 6613 - M18
8-inch x100
Field 40'

K. Glyn Jones

NGC 6633
8½-inch x51
Field 45'

E.S. Barker

IC 4725 - M25
8-inch x40
Field 65'

K. Glyn Jones

WS	Cat	RA	Dec	m	AD	Type	Con
278	NGC 6645	18 31.1	−16 55	8.3	11.0	III 1 m	Sgr

(8) A cloud of very faint stars including a fairly bright triple; about 60 stars in a roundish shape, over three quarters of these being about 12 mag; 11 and 11½ mag outliers extend in all directions, comprising about 30 to 40 additional stars; main body 6', outliers extend this to 10'.

| 279 | NGC 6649 | 18 32.1 | −10 25 | 10.1 | 6.0 | II 2 m | Sct |

Contains the Cepheid V 367 Sct.

(8) Located just NE of a 9 mag star; coarse group about 4' in diameter and roundish; contains 15 to 20 stars of 11 mag and fainter; poor, but quite definite; best at LP.

(6) Faint, nearly 10' across and barely resolved.

| 280 | NGC 6664 | 18 35.4 | −08 15 | 9.0 | 13.5 | III 2 m | Sct |

Contains the Cepheid EV Sct.

(12) 25 stars in 15' field.

(8) Coarse group of mostly faint stars; displays a U-shape, opening to the SW, the majority of stars being at the base of the U; rich main body, about 12' x 6', containing about 30 stars of 10 mag and fainter; alpha Sct (4 mag) lies to the W.

(3) Faint, large and scattered; seems very rich.

| 281 | NGC 6694 | 18 44.0 | −09 25 | 9.3 | 9.0 | I 1 m | Sct |
| | M26 | | | | | | |

The brightest star in this cluster is 11.9 mag.

(12) 20 stars in 10' area, the brightest forming a shape like the northern sky section of Scorpio.

(8) Not very impressive but contains some fairly dense patches of faint stars; the central four brightest stars form a kite shape and two arms of faint stars lie to the N and S.

(6) Rather poor; 4 stars plus slight nebulosity.

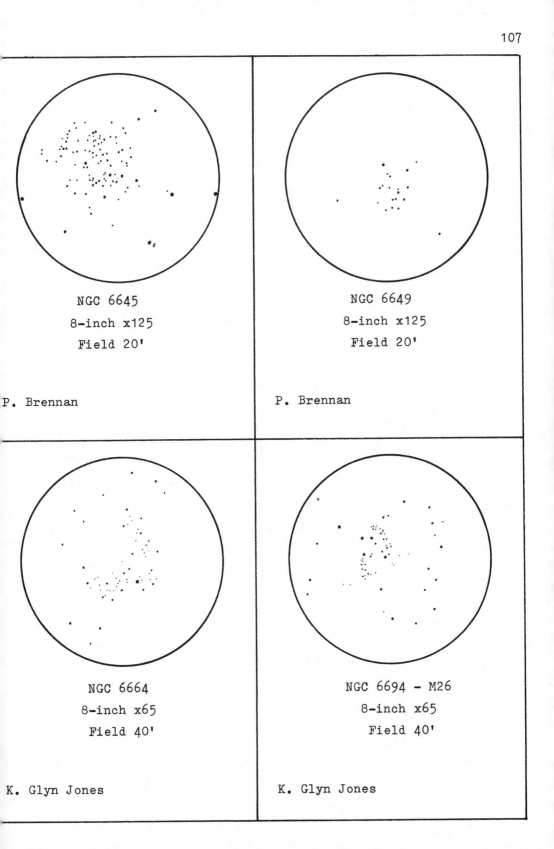

NGC 6645
8-inch x125
Field 20'

P. Brennan

NGC 6649
8-inch x125
Field 20'

P. Brennan

NGC 6664
8-inch x65
Field 40'

K. Glyn Jones

NGC 6694 - M26
8-inch x65
Field 40'

K. Glyn Jones

WS	Cat	RA	Dec	m	AD	Type	Con
282	NGC 6704	18 49.5	-05 14	9.8	5.0	I 3 m	Sct

(6) A small, faint, nebulous cluster about 2' in diameter; some 11 and 12 mag stars are scattered across and around it, giving dimensions of about 4' x 2'; observed at x65.

283	NGC 6705	18 49.7	-06 18	6.3	12.5	I 2 r	Sct
	M11						

Nuc. of Sct OB1. Contains about 600 stars brighter than 14.8 mag.

(12) A beautiful sight, one of the most impressive with this aperture; almost a globular.
(8) An impressive, compact cluster; the densest part in the shape of a fan or arrow-head with an 8 mag star just inside the apex; the densest part is about 10' or 12' diameter.
(6) Shows a starless vacuity and much nebulosity of unresolved stars.

284	NGC 6709	18 50.3	+10 19	7.6	13.0	III 2 m	Aql

(12) 25 stars in 15' field.
(8) Fairly compact, with dark area in the centre; fan shape to the NE; not very impressive.
(6) 15' diameter; contains a fine double.

285	NGC 6716	18 53.1	-19 55	6.7	7.0	IV 1 p	Sgr

This cluster is obscured by 0.4 magnitudes.

(8) 15 stars in 15' field; others suspected.
(3) Bright, easily resolvable.

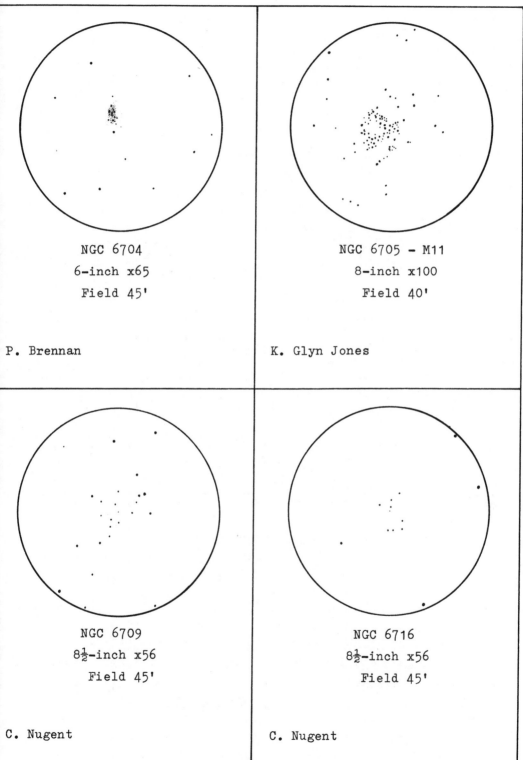

NGC 6704
6-inch x65
Field 45'

P. Brennan

NGC 6705 - M11
8-inch x100
Field 40'

K. Glyn Jones

NGC 6709
8½-inch x56
Field 45'

C. Nugent

NGC 6716
8½-inch x56
Field 45'

C. Nugent

WS	Cat	RA	Dec	m	AD	Type	Con
286	NGC 6738	19 00.2	+11 34	8.5	12.5	IV 2 p	Aql

(8) Diameter from 8' to 12', there being a large
number of outliers which may be cluster or field
stars; the richest clump is roundish and contains
25 mag 9 stars, among them a wide 9 mag pair;
many stars arranged in pairs and strings.
(3) Faint, large and loosely grouped.

| 287 | NGC 6756 | 19 07.4 | +04 37 | 10.6 | 3.5 | I 2 m | Aql |

Possible double with NGC 6755.

(8) The dominant feature is a small, quite bright
nebulous patch only partially resolvable and about
0'.5 in extent; it is set in a group of about 15
12 mag stars that extend to the W and S.

| 288 | NGC 6793 | 19 22.1 | -22 08 | - | - | IV 2 p | Sgr |

(10) A very tight group clustered in the centre of
a fairly sparse field; a small triangle of 10 mag
stars dominates, and several wide pairs are to be
seen; fairly rich and about 13' diameter with 23
stars seen; HP is preferable.

| 289 | NGC 6800 | 19 26.1 | +25 05 | - | - | III 2 p | Vul |

(12) 55 stars in 20' field.
(8) Contains about 30 mag 10 stars in a 10' group;
outliers extend this to nearly 20' and raise the
number of stars to 45 or more, including several
9 and 10 mags; overall the cluster members are quite
bright, the cluster giving the impression that few
additional members would be added by an increase in
aperture.
(15 x 80) Faint, large and rich.

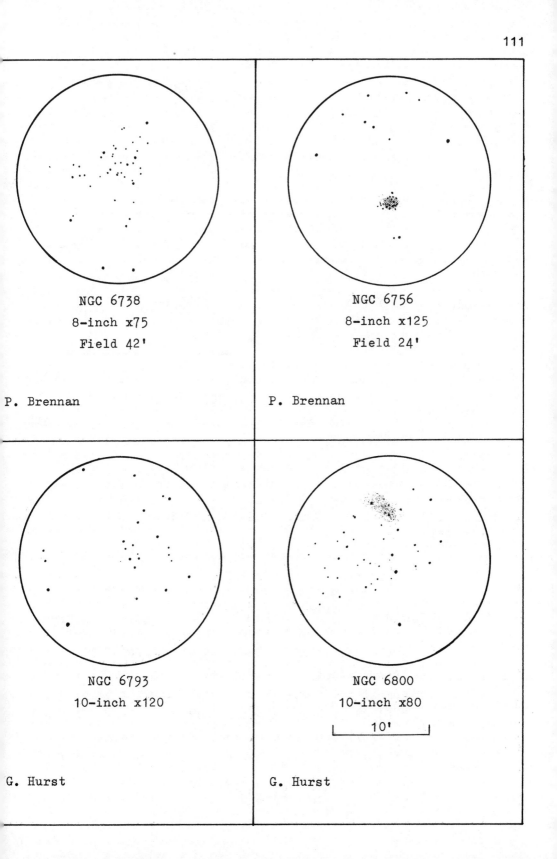

NGC 6738
8-inch x75
Field 42'

P. Brennan

NGC 6756
8-inch x125
Field 24'

P. Brennan

NGC 6793
10-inch x120

G. Hurst

NGC 6800
10-inch x80

|— 10' —|

G. Hurst

WS	Cat	RA	Dec	m	AD	Type	Con
290	Stock 1	19 34.7	+25 09	7.0	60.0	IV 2 p	Vul

(10) Stars scattered across the entire field at x40, but it hardly resembles a cluster; 47 stars in an area of 40', most prominent are two rich groups each containing a number of neat doubles.

| 291 | NGC 6811 | 19 37.4 | +46 30 | 9.9 | 11.5 | III 1 p | Cyg |

(12) 40 stars in 12' area.
(10) A faint cluster rich in two main areas; contains several doubles including one of 10 mag in the E part diameter 10'; 35 stars.
(15 x 80) Faint, very large and rich.

| 292 | NGC 6815 | 19 39.9 | +26 47 | - | - | IV 2 p | Cyg |

(12) 40 stars in 15' x 10' area.
(10) Large but not rich cluster in a superb field; stars of 10 mag and below are scattered throughout the field, which has a noticeable starless area to the SW; cluster stars all appear white; 37 stars.
(15 x 80) Faint, oval object.

| 293 | NGC 6819 | 19 40.5 | +40 08 | 9.9 | 5.2 | I 1 r | Cyg |

Several red giants are members of this cluster, the brightest being variable.

(12) 60 stars in 25' field.
(10) Glittering group of small stars not fully resolved at x120; resolved stars are of 11 to 13 mag set against unresolved nebulosity; roughly U-shaped, small and compact; 21 stars; diameter 5'
(6) Small group of 11 and 12 mag stars; nebulosity visible even in moonlight; 3' to 4' diameter.
(15 x 80) Faint, very rich, tightly grouped.

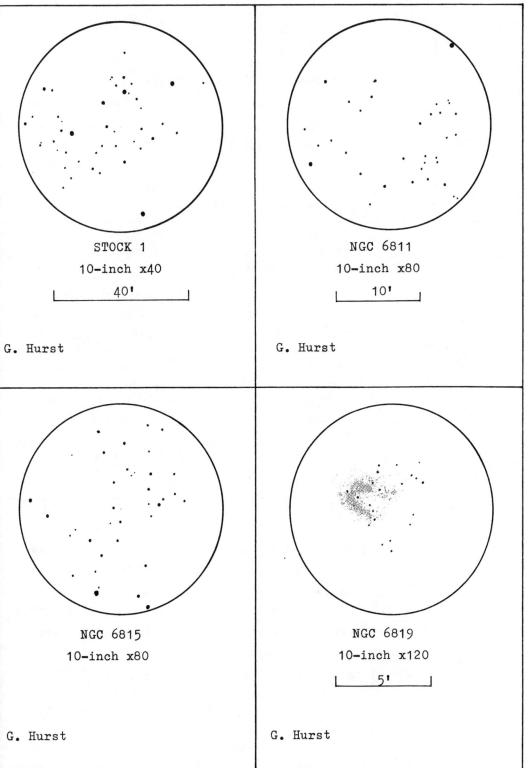

STOCK 1
10-inch x40
40'

G. Hurst

NGC 6811
10-inch x80
10'

G. Hurst

NGC 6815
10-inch x80

G. Hurst

NGC 6819
10-inch x120
5'

G. Hurst

WS	Cat	RA	Dec	m	AD	Type	Con
294	NGC 6823	19 42.1	+23 15	9.8	5.5	I 3 p	Vul

(12) 20 stars in 5' area; in rich 30' field.

(8) Stands out only with averted vision; at the
centre are 3 stars in a row, 1 mag 10 and 2 mag 11;
about 30 10 mag stars in all, plus others of 12 mag;
about 5' x 3' in size.

(6) At times shows a nebulous appearance; contains
quite a number of faint stars.

WS	Cat	RA	Dec	m	AD	Type	Con
295	NGC 6830	19 50.0	+23 01	8.7	6.0	II 2 p	Vul

(12) 20 stars in 7' area.

(8) Main part is irregularly round and about 4' to
5' in extent; contains 5 stars of mag 10 and 11 and
a score of mag 12; x75 fairly rich and compressed.

WS	Cat	RA	Dec	m	AD	Type	Con
296	NGC 6834	19 51.2	+29 21	9.7	5.5	II 2 m	Vul

Contains a number of infrared stars.

(12) 25 stars in 10' area.

(10) Very rich and compressed with inner groupings;
needs a minimum of x120 to resolve, appearing as a
nebulous streak at LP; 43 stars; size 4' x 3'.

WS	Cat	RA	Dec	m	AD	Type	Con
297	NGC 6866	20 02.9	+43 55	9.0	7.0	II 2 m	Cyg

(10) Rich, compact group; 2 bright lines of stars
extend S, and an 11 mag close double is near the
centre; haze of unresolved stars; 21 stars seen.

(8½) Consists mainly of faint stars in fairly tight
formation; several doubles involved, and several
brighter stars in the field.

(6) Fairly bright and small stars with nebulosity.

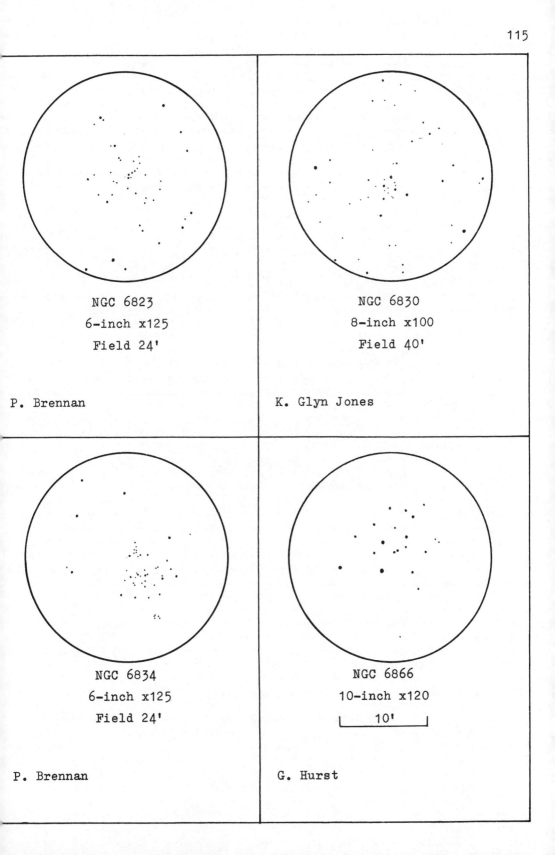

NGC 6823
6-inch x125
Field 24'

P. Brennan

NGC 6830
8-inch x100
Field 40'

K. Glyn Jones

NGC 6834
6-inch x125
Field 24'

P. Brennan

NGC 6866
10-inch x120

10'

G. Hurst

WS	Cat	RA	Dec	m	AD	Type	Con
298	NGC 6871	20 04.9	+35 42	6.0	30.0	IV 3 p	Cyg

Contains a number of infrared stars.

- -

(10) Consists of 2 bright doubles with all the other stars much fainter plus some haze of unresolved stars contains the double Σ 2630, a yellow pair of 7 mag. 16 stars; 10' diameter.

(8) x170 55 stars in 20' area; several multiple stars

299	IC 1311	20 09.5	+41 08	13.1	63.0	II 3 r	Cyg

- -

(10) Very small, faint, compact group with a glow in the background suggesting a rich object; very difficu 13 stars at x120; 6' diameter.

(8½) x116 and x232 a star of 12 mag accompanied by on of 13 mag a little to the NW and enveloped in nebulos

300	NGC 6883	20 10.3	+35 46	8.3	11.5	I 3 p	Cyg

- -

(12) 40 stars in 15' area; rich field.

(10) Compact group consisting of a bright 10 mag doub with an arrow of stars to the E; fairly rich in a qui dense field; 21 stars; 12' diameter.

(8½) About 15' diameter consisting of white stars of about 9 to 11 mag; no nebulosity in the area, but the are several bright double stars to be seen.

301	NGC 6885	20 10.9	+26 24	9.1	7.0	III 2 p	Vul

Superimposed upon NGC 6882.

- -

(10) Bright, with yellow 20 Vul (6 mag) at the centre contains rich and barren areas.

(8) x170 the two clusters 6' apart, the separation being somewhat arbitrary; 15 stars seen in 6882 and 30 stars in 6885.

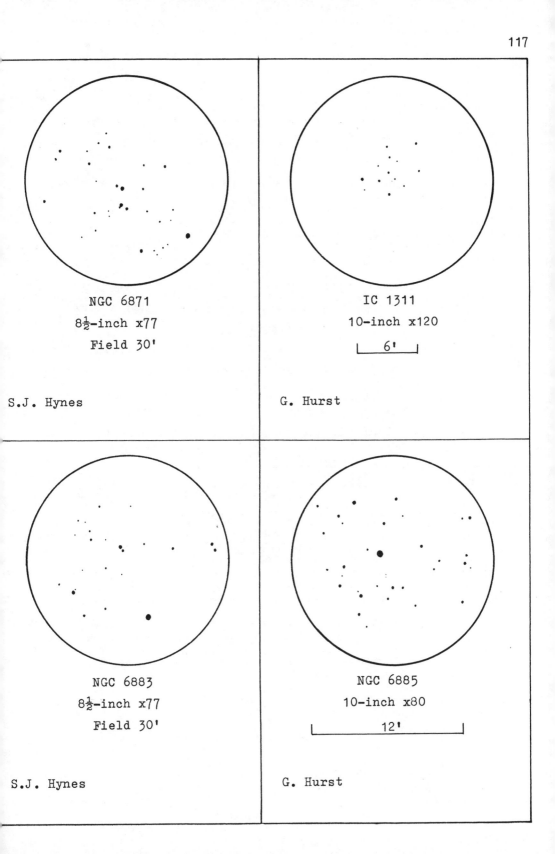

NGC 6871
8½-inch x77
Field 30'

S.J. Hynes

IC 1311
10-inch x120
└ 6' ┘

G. Hurst

NGC 6883
8½-inch x77
Field 30'

S.J. Hynes

NGC 6885
10-inch x80
└ 12' ┘

G. Hurst

WS	Cat	RA	Dec	m	AD	Type	Con
302	Rup 172	20 10.9	+35 33	–	4.0	I 3 p	Cyg

(10) Triangle of 11 mag stars with rays of stars
extending from points of the triangle; a 12 mag
double lies in the W part; no stars are within the
triangle to a limiting magnitude of 14 mag; in the
same LP field as NGC 6883; 21 stars; 5' diameter.

| 303 | IC 4996 | 20 15.5 | +37 33 | 7.2 | 5.6 | I 3 p | Cyg |

(10) Semi-circle of stars showing nebulous at LP;
x120 elongated haze in a fine field; a 9 mag star
is on the N edge; 20 stars.
(8½) A beautiful cluster in a rich field; it consists
of 3 mag 9 stars, the central one being slightly
orange in colour; trailing to the SE of these is a
misty string of faint stars, the brightest being of
about mag 12; the whole cluster seems to be in a
faint envelope of nebulosity.

| 304 | Cr 419 | 20 17.2 | +40 38 | 5.4 | 4.0 | IV 2 g | Cyg |

(10) Compact, but not rich; situated just to the N
of the double Σ 2666; contains stars of 10 to 13 mag,
including an 11 and 12 mag double; 14 stars.

| 305 | Dol 5 | 20 19.6 | +39 18 | – | 7.0 | IV 2 p | Cyg |

(10) Very faint cluster enclosed by a trapezium of
10 mag stars; members are evenly distributed and of
11 mag and below.

119

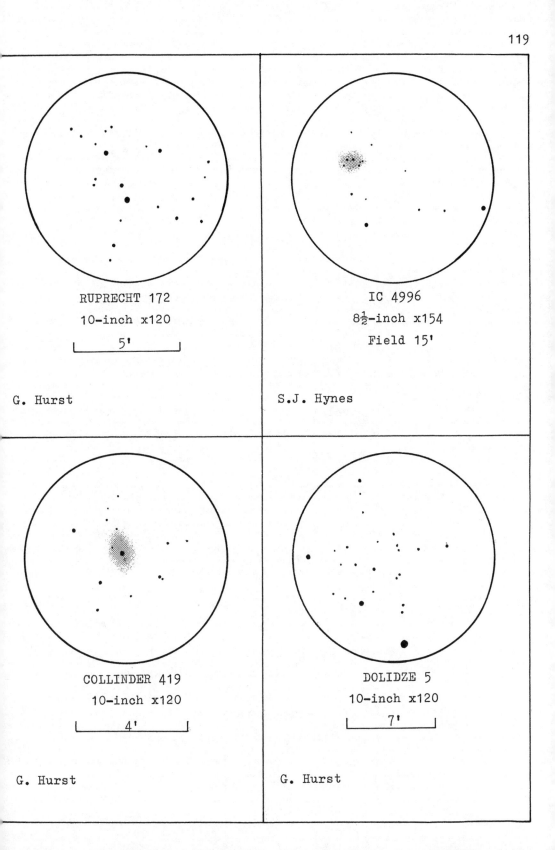

RUPRECHT 172
10-inch x120
5'

G. Hurst

IC 4996
8½-inch x154
Field 15'

S.J. Hynes

COLLINDER 419
10-inch x120
4'

G. Hurst

DOLIDZE 5
10-inch x120
7'

G. Hurst

WS	Cat	RA	Dec	m	AD	Type	Con
306	Cr 421	20 22.4	+41 37	9.9	6.0	III 1 p	Cyg

(10) 10 mag triangular group with fainter stars to
the W; moderately rich; no doubles; 18 stars.

307	NGC 6910	20 22.2	+40 42	7.7	11.0	I 2 p	Cyg

Related to Cyg OB1.

(10) Bright, loose group containing 2 prominent stars
joined by a line of fainter ones; 14 stars.
(8) Coarse cluster with a peculiar branched shape;
dominated by 2 mag 9 stars, both deep yellow-orange
in colour; about 20 mag 9 stars are included and the
remainder are of mag 11 with a few fainter ones; the
main body is elongated W-E; stands out well in field.

308	NGC 6913	20 23.0	+38 27	9.1	7.0	III 3 p	Cyg
	M29						

This cluster contains a number of infrared stars and
is obscured by 3 magnitudes. 6 stars brighter than
9.5 mag. Diffuse nebulosity lies around.

(12) Disappointing; only a few stars in a loose group
(8) Very sparse, consisting of 7 or 8 fairly bright
stars, the 4 brightest forming a quadrilateral and
another 3 a small triangle to the N; only a few other
faint stars are in the vicinity.
(6) 5' diameter; contains a red star.

309	NGC 6939	20 30.9	+60 33	10.2	7.0	I 1 m	Cep

(16½) Large, rich group with the brightest members
in the SW end, which is the densest part.
(10) Irregular shape with the W and S ends the most
distinct; few stars resolved, the remainder showing
as a greyish glow; in a poor field.
(8) 5 mag 11 stars and many fainter; diffuse to the E
overall shape like a kite.

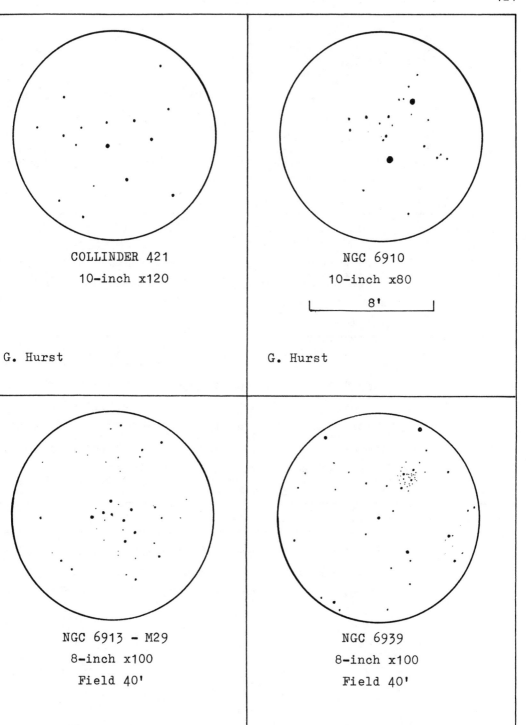

COLLINDER 421

10-inch x120

G. Hurst

NGC 6910

10-inch x80

8'

G. Hurst

NGC 6913 - M29

8-inch x100

Field 40'

K. Glyn Jones

NGC 6939

8-inch x100

Field 40'

K. Glyn Jones

WS	Cat	RA	Dec	m	AD	Type	Con
310	NGC 6940	20 33.5	+28 13	7.1	32.5	III 2 m	Vul

(10) Rich, bright group with a compressed area S of a 10 mag red star at the centre; contains many doubles and triples.
(8½) Major axis in PA 160° - 340°; densely populated in the S part; 91 stars.
(8) 50 stars in 45' field; faint.

311	Rup 173	20 40.8	+35 27	-	50.0	III 2 p	Cyg

(10) A very large, loose, coarse group; the brighter stars cover an area about 20' across, but few stars are brighter than 13 mag; 50 stars in a LP field and 34 stars in the cluster region.

312	Rup 174	20 42.5	+36 57	-	5.0	II 2 p	Cyg

(10) The X on the chart opposite shows the position of this cluster, which is therefore beyond the reach of this aperture; the field itself is of interest, containing a double star marked A in the chart, both stars are about equal and white in colour; the field displays star-poor regions.

313	Rup 175	20 44.2	+35 25	-	9.0	III 2 p	Cyg

(10) Irregular semi-circle of stars enclosing a star-less area; not a rich group; a 13 mag double lies on the SW edge; 27 stars at x120.

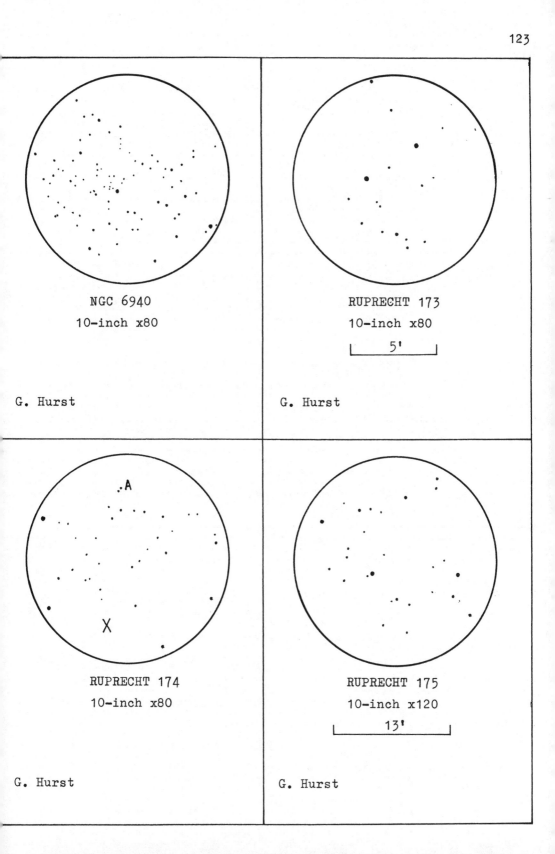

NGC 6940
10-inch x80

G. Hurst

RUPRECHT 173
10-inch x80
5'

G. Hurst

RUPRECHT 174
10-inch x80

G. Hurst

RUPRECHT 175
10-inch x120
13'

G. Hurst

WS	Cat	RA	Dec	m	AD	Type	Con
314	NGC 7063	21 23.4	+36 23	8.9	12.0	III 2 p	Cyg

(10) A generally bright cluster containing stars of 10 to 12 mag which are fairly loose and evenly distributed; a pair of stars at 'A' on the chart opposite resolved at x120, 12 and 12.5 mag and very close; 18 stars; 7' diameter.

(8) 35 stars in 20' area; very bright.

WS	Cat	RA	Dec	m	AD	Type	Con
315	NGC 7082	21 28.5	+46 59	-	25.0	IV 2 p	Cyg

(8½) Moderate size, about 8'; consists of a mixture of bright and faint white stars of 10 to 13 mag; one or two doubles.

(8) Pretty scattered with about 8 bright stars in a straggling group of fainter ones; not very different from the background.

WS	Cat	RA	Dec	m	AD	Type	Con
316	NGC 7086	21 29.7	+51 29	11.6	6.0	II 2 m	Cyg

(8) A small, fairly isolated cluster containing few bright stars but many faint ones; about 10' diameter; not very impressive.

WS	Cat	RA	Dec	m	AD	Type	Con
317	NGC 7092 M39	21 31.3	+48 20	5.1	32.0	III 2 p	Cyg

Contains about 20 stars between 7 and 10 mag.

(8) Very large group, but rather sparse; 3 stars of mag 8 lie at the corners of a large, almost equi-lateral triangle with the S side aligned E-W; many stars in pairs including a bright pair near the centr lies in a very rich region.

(10 x 50) Very bright and large; resolvable.

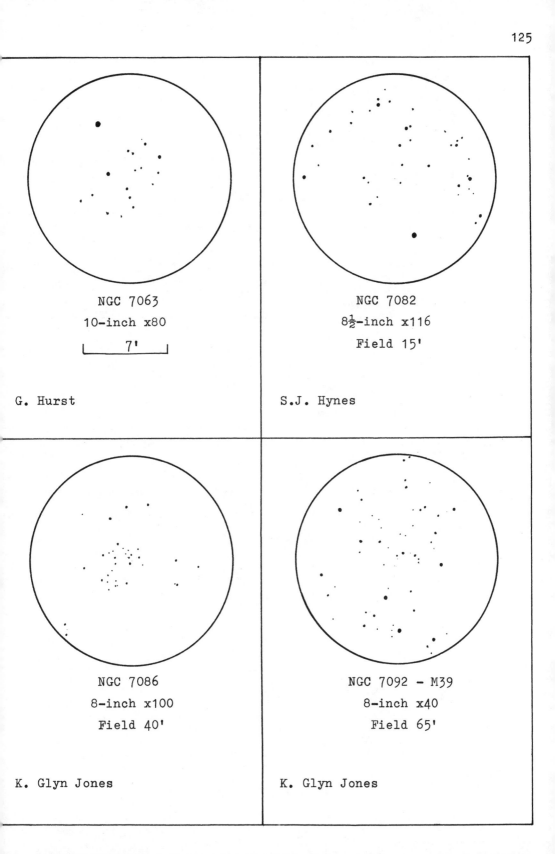

NGC 7063
10-inch x80
|____ 7' ____|

G. Hurst

NGC 7082
8½-inch x116
Field 15'

S.J. Hynes

NGC 7086
8-inch x100
Field 40'

K. Glyn Jones

NGC 7092 – M39
8-inch x40
Field 65'

K. Glyn Jones

WS	Cat	RA	Dec	m	AD	Type	Con
318	NGC 7127	21 43.0	+54 30	–	2.8	IV 2 p	Cyg

(12) 10 stars in 2' area.

(10) Compact group showing considerable haze of the unresolved members; stars of 10 to 13 mag; 8 stars.

(6) 5 faint stars and nebulosity; very small.

WS	Cat	RA	Dec	m	AD	Type	Con
319	NGC 7128	21 43.2	+53 36	11.4	2.5	II 3 m	Cyg

(12) Unresolved except for 4 stars; 3' diameter.

(10) Small, nebulous patch with 5 stars embedded; a 9 mag star on the SE edge.

WS	Cat	RA	Dec	m	AD	Type	Con
320	NGC 7142	21 45.3	+65 41	9.6	7.5	II 2 r	Cep

(6) A round cluster, quite rich, but with all its members very faint; more than 25 stars evenly distributed in an 8' area; a 9 or 10 mag star lies on the N edge; a difficult group.

WS	Cat	RA	Dec	m	AD	Type	Con
321	NGC 7160	21 53.0	+62 39	6.3	5.0	II 3 p	Cep

(12) 15 stars in 10' area; one double, one triple.

(10) Triangle of stars at the centre including 2 star of mag 8; haze of unresolved stars.

(8½) 25 stars; brightest trend E-W.

(6) About 7' diameter; 2 mag 8 stars, 5 of mag 9 to 10 and several of 11 to 12 mag.

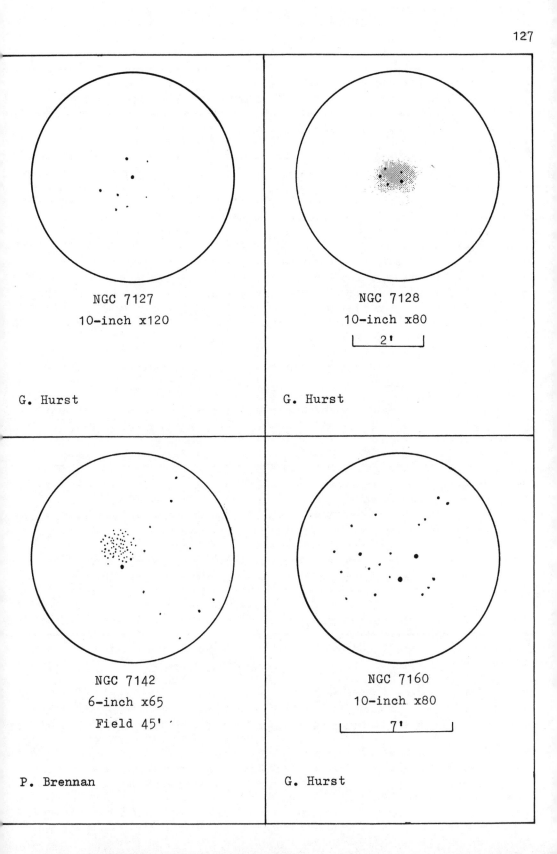

NGC 7127

10-inch x120

G. Hurst

NGC 7128

10-inch x80

L___2'___J

G. Hurst

NGC 7142

6-inch x65

Field 45'

P. Brennan

NGC 7160

10-inch x80

L_____7'_____J

G. Hurst

WS	Cat	RA	Dec	m	AD	Type	Con
322	NGC 7209	22 04.2	+46 22	8.4	16.5	III 1 p	Lac

(12) x80 50 stars in 20' area.

(8½) Difficult to define the borders; sparse star distribution to the S ending in a starless lane; a yellow star lies to the N and a few faint pairs are to be seen; majority of stars are 9 to 10 mag.

(8) Distinct cluster with few bright stars but very many 9, 10 and 11 mag; rather straggling.

(6) About 15' diameter; stars with nebulosity.

WS	Cat	RA	Dec	m	AD	Type	Con
323	IC 1434	22 09.7	+52 42	9.6	6.0	II 1 p	Cyg

(10) A very faint, medium size cluster containing interesting groups of very faint stars in groups, in particular a 13 mag group of a few close stars on the N edge; considerable haze evident, possibly nebulous in parts; situated in a glorious region; diameter 7'; 21 stars seen.

WS	Cat	RA	Dec	m	AD	Type	Con
324	NGC 7235	22 11.7	+57 09	9.4	4.0	III 2 p	Cep

(60) 25 stars in 3' area plus some outliers.

(10) Small group consisting of a triangle of 1 mag 8 and 2 mag 9 stars plus another 8 fainter ones; some haze of unresolved members also evident.

(6) x96 a 9 mag yellow star at the E end; other stars 10 and 11 mag; 4' x 3' diameter.

WS	Cat	RA	Dec	m	AD	Type	Con
325	NGC 7243	22 14.3	+49 45	6.8	30.0	IV 2 p	Lac

Contains eight possible spectroscopic binary stars.

(12) 80 stars in 22' x 16' area; like two clusters; double star with equal white components near centre.

(8½) Triangular shape with points to the NE, NW and S; red star to the N of the central double; a starless lane runs NW to SE; 69+ stars; 30' diameter.

(15 x 80) Large, bright and rich; easily resolvable.

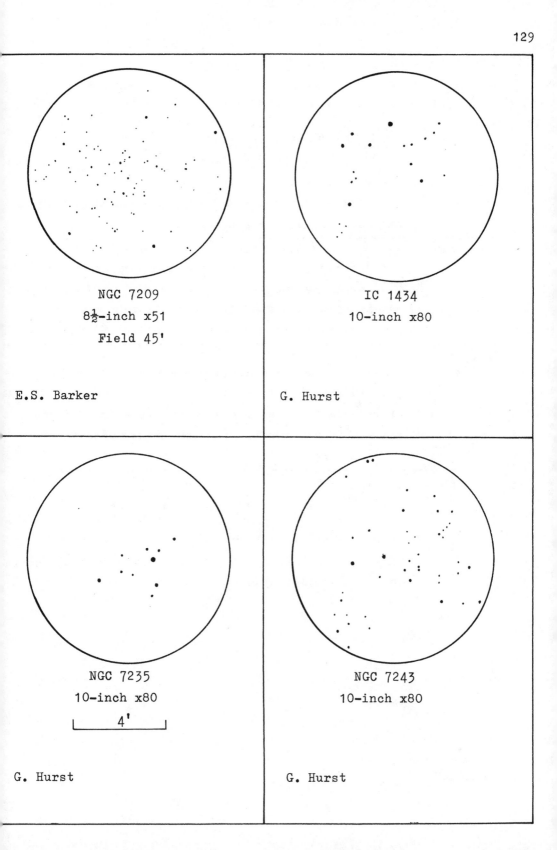

NGC 7209

8½-inch x51

Field 45'

E.S. Barker

IC 1434

10-inch x80

G. Hurst

NGC 7235

10-inch x80

|———— 4' ————|

G. Hurst

NGC 7243

10-inch x80

G. Hurst

WS	Cat	RA	Dec	m	AD	Type	Con
326	NGC 7245	22 14.5	+54 12	11.5	5.0	II 1 p	Lac

(12) Several groupings; richest 15 stars in 6' area.
(10) Very faint and containing some haze; only a few
stars resolved, the brightest to the S.
(8½) Triangle of 8, 9 and 10 mag stars with fainter
ones suspected; 6 stars only seen.

327	IC 1442	22 15.4	+53 54	–	–	II 2 m	Lac

(10) A clustering of faint stars surrounding a 8 mag
reddish star and one of 9 mag; not rich and easy to
overlook during a sweep; x80 20 stars; 9' diameter.

328	NGC 7261	22 19.5	+57 58	9.8	6.0	III 1 p	Cep

(12) 15 stars in 6' area.
(10) Compact, appearing as a double star of 8 and 9
mag at LP; 8 stars in all seen at x80 with fainter
members unresolved.

329	NGC 7281	22 23.8	+57 43	–	–	IV 2 p	Cep

Doubtful whether this is an actual cluster.

(12) 20 stars in 10' area; faint.
(10) A large, bright cluster but not very rich; chain
of 3 mag 8 stars prominent; 18 stars in all.

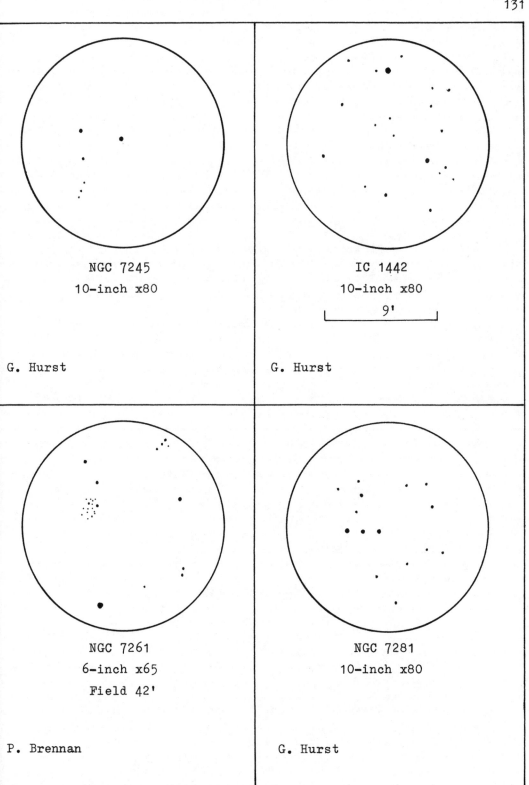

NGC 7245
10-inch x80

G. Hurst

IC 1442
10-inch x80

|_____ 9' _____|

G. Hurst

NGC 7261
6-inch x65
Field 42'

P. Brennan

NGC 7281
10-inch x80

G. Hurst

WS	Cat	RA	Dec	m	AD	Type	Con
330	NGC 7296	22 27.2	+52 10	10.0	4.5	III 2 p	Lac

(12) 15 stars in 4' area.

(10) Lies between an 8 and 9 mag star; extended in a N-S line with 2 curves of faint stars at the centre x80 16 stars; 8' diameter; in a very rich region.

(8½) A small, rather inconspicuous cluster, a little difficult to locate in a rich field; about 5' diam. and consists of 11 to 13 mag stars led by a 9 mag one a distinct nebulous glow of unresolved stars surround.

| 331 | NGC 7380 | 22 46.0 | +57 58 | 8.8 | 8.0 | III 3 p | Cep |

The stars in this cluster emit polarised light due to the presence of intervening interstellar dust.

(12) 20 stars in 20' area; very symmetrical.

(10) Faint, rich group with primary an 8 mag yellow star; 13 mag double on S edge; stars set against a background glow; 26 stars.

| 332 | NGC 7510 | 23 10.5 | +60 26 | 9.6 | 2.5 | II 2 m | Cep |

(12) 10 bright stars and many fainter; 3' diameter.

(10) Distinctly oblong patch of haze at LP; very small and rich; contains a red 10 mag star.

(6) Shows as 2 stars and nebulosity at LP; 2' diam.

| 333 | Mark 50 | 23 14.2 | +60 20 | | 1.5 | I 2 p | Cas |

Consists of the visual binary HD 219460 (WN+BO, $V = 10.03$, separation about 1"). This is surrounded by a compact group of early-type stars. The age of the cluster is about 10^7 yr.

(10) Appears as a nebulous star at LP; at x120 only a few members visible above 13 mag, and it is clearly a highly compressed object; 13 stars, 3' diameter.

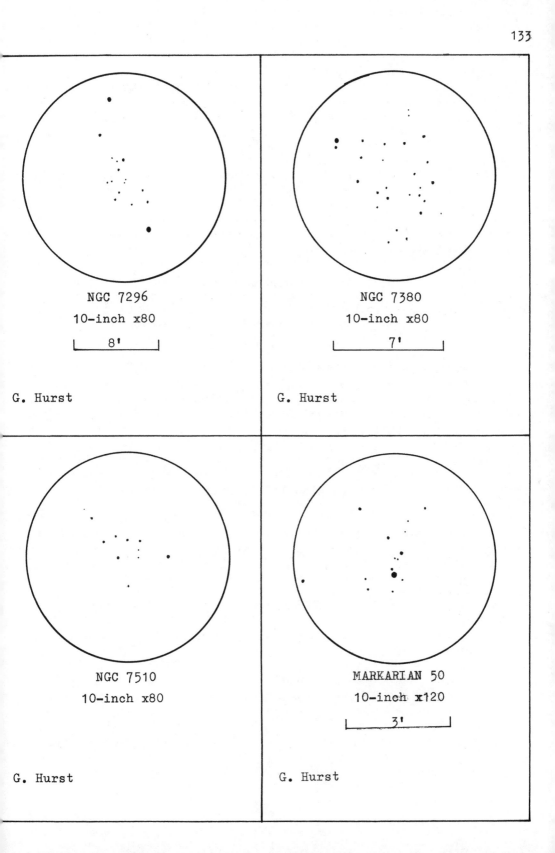

NGC 7296
10-inch x80
⊢——— 8' ———⊣

G. Hurst

NGC 7380
10-inch x80
⊢——— 7' ———⊣

G. Hurst

NGC 7510
10-inch x80

G. Hurst

MARKARIAN 50
10-inch x120
⊢——— 3' ———⊣

G. Hurst

WS	Cat	RA	Dec	m	AD	Type	Con
334	NGC 7654	23 23.1	+61 27	7.3	13.0	I 2 r	Cas
	M52						

Contains about 190 stars of 11 mag and fainter.

- -

(12) 20 stars in 10' area; bright.

(8) Small group containing a few concentrations of faint stars and an 8 mag orange star; inconspicuous

(15 x 80) A few stars resolved; extension to NE.

WS	Cat	RA	Dec	m	AD	Type	Con
335	NGC 7788	23 55.5	+61 15	9.5	7.0	I 2 p	Cas

- -

(10) Rich, compressed group showing considerable haze; difficult to resolve; 8 stars; 4' diameter.

(8½) About 2' across and centred on a 9 mag star; six stars within the group enveloped in a dense nebulosity which is almost resolved.

(15 x 80) Faint, opaque cloud.

WS	Cat	RA	Dec	m	AD	Type	Con
336	NGC 7789	23 55.8	+56 35	9.3	13.5	II 1 r	Cas

About 200 stars, 34% in the central region.

- -

(10) Very large, faint star cloud showing as a luminous glow at LP; difficult to fully resolve; at x80 brighter members only resolved against a rich background of haze; very rich and compressed at the centre; 33 stars; 20' diameter.

WS	Cat	RA	Dec	m	AD	Type	Con
337	NGC 7790	23 57.2	+61 04	7.2	16.5	III 2 p	Cas

Contains Cepheids CE Cas a & b and CF Cas.

- -

(10) Arrow-head shape pointing NNE; the S end is formed by a square of stars and a 13 mag triangle of stars lies on the E edge; 15 stars seen.

(8½) Small group containing stars of 10 to 13 mag; enveloped in nebulosity which is concentrated in particular towards the E side; 11 stars clearly seen including a close double.

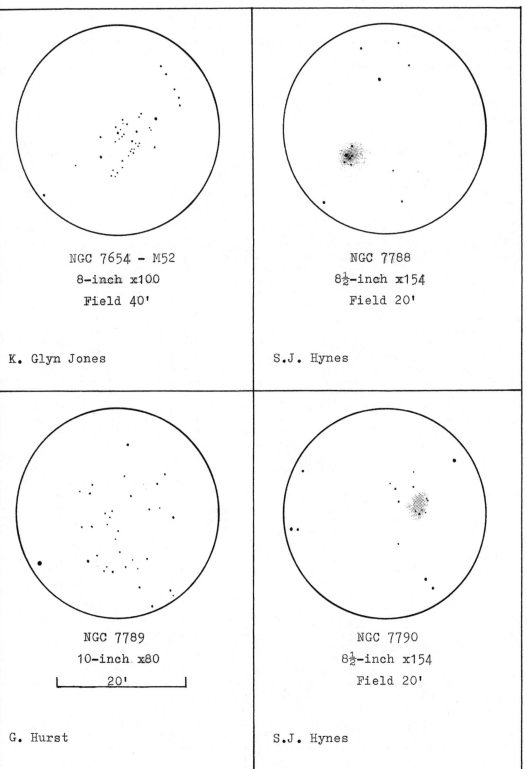

NGC 7654 – M52
8-inch x100
Field 40'

K. Glyn Jones

NGC 7788
8½-inch x154
Field 20'

S.J. Hynes

NGC 7789
10-inch x80
20'

G. Hurst

NGC 7790
8½-inch x154
Field 20'

S.J. Hynes

A Catalogue of Open Clusters.

Part Two : Descriptions of a Further 29 Open Clusters.

WS	Cat	RA	Dec	m	AD	Type	Con
338	NGC 103	00 23.9	+61 12	10.8	4.5	II 2 p	Cas

Nuc. of Cas OB4. Contains emission-line stars.

- -

(8) 30 stars in 40' field, most lying centrally.

(10 x 80) Stands out clearly, although situated in a field of many clusters.

339	NGC 133	00 29.7	+63 13	9.1	7.5	IV 1 p	Cas

Nuc. of Cas OB4.

- -

(10) 9 stars in extended grouping; major axis about 170° - 350°; 10 mag close double near the centre.

(8) 15 stars in 10'; probably fainter stars too; 13' SE lies NGC 146.

(10 x 80) Combines into a large cluster complex with NGC 146.

340	NGC 146	00 31.6	+63 08	9.5	6.0	IV 3 p	Cas

Contains emission-line stars.

- -

(10) 13 stars in 8' diameter group; contains a 10 mag double; major axis in a N-W line; fine fields in the region of this cluster and NGC 133.

(8) 15 stars in 10' area; twin of 133 but fainter.

341	Mel 15	02 30.6	+61 19	6.6	21.0	III 3 p	Cas

This cluster is immersed in emission nebulosity, whic is IC 1805, and is about 120' x 120' in diameter. $H\alpha$ photographs show a loop of emission surrounding the cluster, identified with the radio source W4. Mel 15 is obscured by about 3.8 magnitudes.

- -

($8\frac{1}{2}$) Scattered, with the richest part at the centre where there is an oval ring of 19 stars; the ring is about 5' x 2'.5 in size; no nebulosity seen.

(6) A group of bright stars and about 35 fainter ones rich towards the centre; about 20' diameter.

WS	Cat	RA	Dec	m	AD	Type	Con
42	NGC 956	02 31.1	+44 33	9.2	7.5	IV 1 p	And

(6) Lies between a pair of 9 or 10 mag stars, and
extends more to the northern of these; most members
are faint, and the main part is formed by an arc of
5 stars running alongside the E side of the pair of
stars mentioned above; about 6' x 3' in size, and
appears slightly nebulous at LP.

| 43 | NGC 1444 | 03 47.5 | +52 35 | 6.4 | 3.0 | IV 1 p | Per |

Contains the double star Σ 446.

(12) 15 stars in 15' field; not impressive.
(8) Surrounds a double star with a 9 mag primary; the
cluster is about 3' x 2' in extent and elongated NW-
SE; contains no more than 10 stars, all 12 mag and
fainter; a coarse, poor and small object.

| 44 | Hyades | 04 25.0 | +15 53 | 0.8 | 320.0 | I 3 m | Tau |

The Taurus Moving Cluster. The distance to this group
has recently been revised, and is now put at a figure
of about 40 pc.

Being a large, loose group, the Hyades was not the
subject of any telescopic observations, binoculars
being the ideal instruments to use for its study;
too well-known for any description; due to its size
and nearness, it is an easy naked-eye object.

| 45 | NGC 1624 | 04 38.4 | +50 24 | 11.8 | 1.9 | I 2 p N | Per |

Connected with emission nebulosity.

(8) Consists of an 11 mag star and about 6 mag 12
ones; surrounded by nebulosity, both this and the
cluster being elongated NW-SE; nebulosity 3' diam.

WS	Cat	RA	Dec	m	AD	Type	Con
346	NGC 1746	05 02.1	+23 47	6.2	42.5	III 1 p	Tau

(12) 50 stars in an irregular group; about 25' across
with some outliers.

(10) More concentrated on the E side; rich clustering
and a dense centre; 54 stars including a quadruple of
1 mag 10 and 3 mag 13.

(8) 30 bright stars in a group almost 1° across.

| 347 | NGC 2112 | 05 25.6 | +00 23 | 8.6 | 9.0 | II 3 m | Ori |

Contains about 90 stars of 10 mag and below.

(6) A very coarse, inconspicuous cluster; contains
about 7 to 10 stars of mag 11 and fainter which are
scattered in a region 3' x 1'.5 elongated NW-SE; a
9 mag star lies close to the NW.

| 348 | NGC 2126 | 06 01.0 | +49 54 | 8.8 | 6.6 | II 1 p | Aur |

(12) 15 stars in 15' field.

(8) Loose group of about 10 to 15 stars.

(6) A poor sight, requiring averted vision to be seen;
about 5' in extent and irregular in form; contains 15
mag 11 stars and a mag 6 star lies on the NE edge.

| 349 | NGC 2186 | 06 10.7 | +05 28 | 9.0 | 3.5 | II 2 p | Ori |

(12) Weak group; 25 stars in 15' field.

(6) 11 and 12 mag stars plus fainter; difficult.

| 350 | NGC 2192 | 06 13.4 | +35 52 | 10.9 | 6.0 | III 1 p | Aur |

(14) Faint group in a rich field; all stars resolved.

(8) 20 faint stars in an amorphous group; 10' diam.

(6) About 12 very faint stars evenly scattered across
a slightly nebulous background; in a rich field.

WS	Cat	RA	Dec	m	AD	Type	Con
351	NGC 2250	06 31.5	−05 01	8.9	8.0	IV 2 p	Mon

(6) A small, coarse cluster of faint stars with 12 members of 11 mag and fainter; a 9 mag star lies on the N edge; elongated E-W and about 5' x 4' in size; stands out quite well with averted vision.

WS	Cat	RA	Dec	m	AD	Type	Con
352	NGC 2269	06 42.6	+04 35	10.4	3.5	II 2 p	Mon

(6) Very much elongated, about 3' x 1', and shows as nebulous; an 11 mag star lies at the centre; the nebulosity breaks up into extremely faint stars and a coarse halo of similar stars surrounds the main body; located in a fairly rich field.

WS	Cat	RA	Dec	m	AD	Type	Con
353	NGC 2331	07 05.7	+27 24	8.4	16.5	IV 1 p	Gem

(12) 20 stars in 15' field.
(8) Roughly triangular in shape; most members faint with some of 9 mag; several faint pairs; 15 stars.

WS	Cat	RA	Dec	m	AD	Type	Con
54	NGC 2374	07 22.9	−13 12	7.4	10.0	II 3 p	CMa

(12) 25 stars in 12' field.
(6) Irregular cluster with nebulous region to the S which resolves into faint stars at x120.

WS	Cat	RA	Dec	m	AD	Type	Con
55	NGC 2421	07 35.2	−20 33	8.6	8.0	I 2 m	Pup

(10) Well-defined, fairly rich, compact cluster; 8 fairly bright stars and more fainter ones; 8' diam.

WS	Cat	RA	Dec	m	AD	Type	Con
56	Mel 72	07 36.2	−10 22	9.4	9.0	II 1 p	Pup

(10) A very rich congregation of faint stars; 7' in diameter and irregularly round; stars concentrated towards the centre; very like a globular cluster.

WS	Cat	RA	Dec	m	AD	Type	Con
357	NGC 2453	07 46.7	−27 11	9 4	5.0	I 2 p	Pup

(10½) 20 stars in 4' area; neat group.

(6) A very small cluster of 11 mag and fainter stars triangular in shape and about 2' in extent; x65 only 8 stars resolved; a 9 mag star lies close NW.

358	NGC 2479	07 53.9	−17 39	9.8	9.0	III 1 m	Pup

(12) 30 very faint stars in 10' area.

(10) Made up of approximately 40 rather faint stars, half being only visible with averted vision; at x51 appears nebulous; diameter about 10'.

359	H 2	07 54.3	−25 44	9.0	6.0	II 2 p	Pup

(10½) 40 stars in clumpy groups; 5' across.

360	NGC 6507	17 58.2	−17 23	7.5	7.0	IV 2 p	Sgr

(6) A coarse cluster of 11 mag stars with one of 9 or 10 mag on the S edge; contains about 12 stars in an area 8' x 4' extending NE-SW; not conspicuous.

361	H 19	18 16.1	−13 22	12.1	3.5	I 2 m	Sgr

(8) 8' diameter; a spangle of faint stars.

362	NGC 6755	19 06.5	+04 10	9.5	10.0	IV 2 m	Aql

(8) 2 groups of 10 to 15 stars, each 4' across.

(6) 9 to 11 mag stars plus faint nebulosity.

363	H 20	19 52.0	+18 16	9.5	7.0	II 2 p	Sge

(12) 40 faint stars in 12' area; two centres.

364	NGC 7062	21 22.3	+46 16	11.7	4.5	III 1 p	Cyg

(10) Nebulous at LP; a faint, compact cluster which is extended NW-SE.

WS	Cat	RA	Dec	m	AD	Type	Con
65	NGC 7226	22 09.6	+55 17	13.3	2.5	I 1 p	Cep

Related to Cep-Lac OB1.

- -

(6) x65 a faint nebula, formless and about 1' in extent; it lies SE of the southernmost member of an 11 mag pair; the nebulosity shows slight central brightening, and 2 fairly rich knots of faint stars lie close to the E; in a very rich field.

| 66 | NGC 7762 | 23 48.6 | +67 53 | 10.0 | 11.5 | II 2 p | Cep |

- -

(16½) Rich group, consisting of small stars set in a rectangular shape; major axis NW-SE, and 2 bright stars lie near the N edge.

(6) A coarse cloud of 20 to 25 stars scattered over a 10' x 5' area; a few stars of 11 mag are visible, but most are of 12 mag; near the W end is a very elongated and quite rich group of 11 mag stars which are just resolved at x105 but appear rather nebulous at x65.

LIST OF ADDITIONAL OBJECTS.

In the list of additional objects we have included a number of standard NGC clusters as well as number of small groups and objects associated with nebulosity. Also to be found is NGC 5637, which, although located below the declination limit of this Handbook, is nevertheless an object of interest.

Cluster		RA	Dec	m	AD	Type	Con
Be	59	00 00.7	+67 16		10.0	III 2 p	Cep

The brightest probable member of this cluster is BD+66°1675, V = 9.05.

NGC	136	00 30.1	+61 23		2.0	II 2 p	Cas

Contains 40 to 50 stars between 13 and 18 mag.

Be	4	00 43.6	+64 15		5.0	I 2 p	Cas

The brightest probable member of this cluster is BD+63°89, V = 9.50, a possible Hα emission star.

St	3	01 10.7	+62 12		2.0	IV 1 p	Cas

Contains stars of 11 to 13 mag.

Cr	21	01 48.7	+27 07	8.1	6.0	IV 2 p	Tri

Group of 15 stars; doubtful whether it is a cluster.

Ba	10	02 17.0	+58 12		4.8		Per

No type has been assigned to this group. Contains stars from 11.17 mag and below, the majority being over 13 mag.

Mark	6	02 27.8	+60 32		4.5	IV 2 p	Cas

Contains about 12 stars including an emission-line star associated with nebulosity.

King	4	02 33.9	+58 53		3.0	II 1 p	Cam
Be	65	02 37.1	+60 18		5.0	I 2 p	Cam

The brightest probable member of this cluster is BD+59°524, V = 10.79

IC	361	04 16.9	+58 14	11.2	6.5	II 1 r	Cam

Contains about 40 stars.

NGC	1605	04 33.2	+45 12	11.0	5.0	III 1 m	Per
St	8	05 26.0	+34 24		5.0	I 2 p	Aur

Contains stars of 9 mag and below.

Cr	74	05 47.1	+07 23	14.2	3.0	III 2 p	Ori

List of Additional Objects.

Cluster	RA	Dec	m	AD	Type	Con
IC 2157	06 03.4	+24 00	9.7	4.5	III 2 p	Gem
NGC 2236	06 28.3	+06 51	11.4	3.5	III 2 p	Mon
NGC 2243	06 28.8	−31 16	10.9	3.5	I 2 r	CMa
NGC 2252	06 33.6	+05 24	8.0	7.0	IV 2 p	Mon

Contains about 10 stars of 9 mag and below.

Tr 5	06 35.4	+09 28	10.0	7.0	II 3 r	Mon

A probable member of this cluster is the red carbon star V 493 Mon

Cr 110	06 37.1	+02 03	10.6	12.0	III 1 m	Mon

Contains about 60 stars.

Cr 115	06 45.2	+02 03	9.0	7.5	III 2 p	Mon

Contains about 30 stars.

NGC 2175s	07 09.4	+20 37		1.5		Gem

A small group near NGC 2174-5 (see Section 1 of the catalogue). Contains about 15 stars which are immersed in nebulosity, along with NGC 2174-5, on the Palomar Sky Survey E-print. Part of Gem OB1.

Cr 132a,b	07 13.7	−31 03	3.9	77.5	III 3 p	CMa

132a has a distance of about 560 pc and 132b about 330 pc. The eclipsing binary FF CMa (HD 55173) $7^m.64 - 7^m.84$; p = 0.547385d, is a probable member of 132a.

Ha 8	07 22.3	−12 17		4.2	IV 3 m	CMa

Contains about 35 stars of 12 mag and below.

Tr 6	07 25.0	−24 15	10.0	6.5	III 2 p	Pup

Contains about 22 stars.

NGC 2395	07 25.7	+13 38	9.3	15.0	III 1 p	Gem

Contains about 53 stars of 9 mag and below.

NGC 2420	07 36.9	+21 38	9.8	4.0	I 2 p	Gem
NGC 2455	07 47.9	−21 14	10.1	6.0	III 2 p	Pup
Ha 18c	07 51.4	−26 10			III 1 p	Pup

Possibly not a real cluster.

List of Additional Objects.

Cluster		RA	Dec	m	AD	Type	Con
Ha	18a	07 51.5	−26 10		1.1	I 3 pN	Pup

Contains about 18 stars of 11 mag and below.

Ha	18b	07 51.5	−26 10		1.0	II 3 pN	Pup

Contains about 7 stars of 12 mag and below.

Ha	19	07 51.7	−28 23		1.8	I 3 pN	Pup

Contains about 25 stars of 14 mag and below.

NGC 2482		07 53.9	−24 14	8.8	11.0	III 1 m	Pup

Ha	20	07 55.0	−30 12		1.8	II 3 p	Pup

Contains stars of 14 mag and below.

NGC 2489		07 55.2	−30 00	9.2	8.5	II 2 m	Pup

Rup	44	07 58.1	−28 23		5.0	III 1 p	Pup

Contains about 100 OB stars of 12 mag and below.
This cluster and the Ha 18 groups are probably part
of a distant spiral arm which is situated at about
6.8 kpc from the Sun.

Ha	21	08 00.1	−26 58		1.1	II 1 p	Pup

Contains stars of 15 mag and below. This cluster
shows low reddening while Ha 20 is highly reddened,
indicating the tendency of the interstellar dust to
lie below the galactic plane in Puppis.

NGC 2533		08 06.0	−29 47	10.1	2.5	III 1 p	Pup

NGC 2548		08 12.4	−05 43	5.2	54.0	I 2 m	Hya

Contains about 130 stars from 9 to 13 mag.

NGC 2571		08 17.9	−29 40	7.4	11.0	IV 1 p	Pup

NGC 2587		08 22.3	−29 25	9.2	7.5	II 1 p	Pup

NGC 2627		08 36.2	−29 51	8.5	9.5	III 2 p	Pyx

NGC 5367		13 56.2	−39 51				Cen

NGC 5367 is a reflection nebula in which lies a
young cluster associated with the head of cometary
globule 12. One of the two most luminous stars is
possibly connected with the transient X-ray source
A1353-40. NGC 5367 may lie inside an H I loop, and
star formation may have been triggered by a supernova
explosion about 10^7 yr ago. Absorption 1 magnitude.

List of Additional Objects.

Cluster	RA	Dec	m	AD	Type	Con
IC 1257	17 25.8	−07 02				Oph

Classification uncertain. No data available.

Cluster	RA	Dec	m	AD	Type	Con
Tr 27	17 34.1	−33 26	9.1	8.0	I 2 p	Sco

A heavily reddened young cluster containing red and
blue supergiant stars. The extinction across the
face of the cluster varies from 3 to 8 magnitudes.

Cluster	RA	Dec	m	AD	Type	Con
NGC 6469	17 51.4	−22 20	8.4	12.0	III 2 p	Sgr
NGC 6520	18 01.9	−27 54	7.2	6.0	I 2 m	Sgr

A young cluster including three stars which
illuminate a reflection nebula. Two of the stars in
the nebulosity are heavily reddened, and the mean
absorption is 0.37 magnitudes.

Cluster	RA	Dec	m	AD	Type	Con
NGC 6540	18 04.8	−27 49	14.6	0.5	III 1 p	Sgr

Contains about 20 stars.

Cluster	RA	Dec	m	AD	Type	Con
NGC 6546	18 05.7	−23 19	8.5	12.0	III 2 m	Sgr

Contains about 45 stars.

Cluster	RA	Dec	m	AD	Type	Con
NGC 6583	18 14.3	−22 09	11.9	2.5	II 1 m	Sgr
Tr 33	18 23.3	−19 42	9.0	5.0	II 3 m	Sgr
Tr 34	18 38.5	−08 31	11.6	8.0	II 2 m	Sct
	19 43.2	+27 42				Vul

A small cluster of 7 or 8 faint stars embedded in
the dark nebula Lynds 810. The main part of the
cloud is about 10' x 7'

Cluster	RA	Dec	m	AD	Type	Con
Ros 4	20 02.3	+29 00				Vul

No data known about this cluster except that it is
possibly connected with IC 4954-5, a reddened
reflection nebula.

Cluster	RA	Dec	m	AD	Type	Con
Biur 2	20 08.3	+35 24	13.0		III 2 p	Cyg

Related to nucleus of Cyg OB1.

Cluster	RA	Dec	m	AD	Type	Con
Be 86	20 19.3	+38 36	8.0		I 3 p	Cyg

The brightest probable member of this cluster is
HDE 228969, V = 9.50.

Cluster	RA	Dec	m	AD	Type	Con
Be 87	20 20.6	+37 16	8.0		IV 2 p	Cyg

The brightest probable member of this cluster is
HDE 229059, V = 8.70. The variable V 439 Cyg
($12^m.6 - 13^m.0$, p = 260d) lies near the cluster centre.

List of Additional Objects.

Cluster	RA	Dec	m	AD	Type	Con
NGC 7023	21 00.2	+68 04	7.1	5.0		Cyg
Ba 13	21 10.1	+46 22		10.0		Cyg

Contains about 100 stars.

Ba 12	21 10.4	+45 54		6.0		Cyg

Contains about 75 stars.

Ba 14	21 21.7	+44 34		12.0		Cyg

Contains about 107 stars and is probably a small star cloud and not a stellar group.

Ba 15	21 22.6	+48 10				Cyg

Contains 46 probable members, the majority being concentrated in an area of 36 sq. arcminutes.

NGC 7067	21 23.3	+47 54	13.0	2.5	II 2 p	Cyg
Tr 37	21 38.3	+57 22	5.1	50.0	II 3 m	Cep

Nucleus of Cep OB2. Contains about 30 stars, a number showing emission-lines, and is associated with the bright and dark nebulosity IC 1396

NGC 7129	21 40.7	+65 59	11.3	1.25		Cep

Contains about 7 stars and associated nebulosity.

IC 5146	21 52.2	+47 09	8.3	9.5	IV 2 pN	Cyg

A cluster of about 12 stars connected with the bright and dark nebulosity known as the Cocoon Nebula. The total mass of associated dust is about 4.5 M_0.

Be 94	22 21.8	+55 43		4.0	I 1 p	Lac

This cluster is obscured by 2 magnitudes.

NGC 7419	22 53.3	+60 42	13.1	2.5	II 3 r	Cep

Contains the infrared star IRC+60375, an M7 supergiant. The cluster is obscured by 4.5 magnitudes.

King 10	22 54.4	+59 02		3.0	II 3 m	Cep

Contains a number of emission-line stars.

King 20	23 32.1	+58 22		5.0	II 1 p	Cas
King 12	23 51.8	+61 49		2.0	I 2 p	Cas

Contains about 27 stars from 10 to 16 mag.

PART FOUR : A CATALOGUE OF GLOBULAR CLUSTERS.

INTRODUCTION.

The catalogue contains observations of 63 globular clusters made by 11 observers using telescopes of 40 to 3-inches aperture and 15 x 80, 20 x 50 and 7 x 35 binoculars. The observations are divided into two sections comprising a) descriptions and field drawings of 53 clusters and b) descriptions of a further 10 objects for which no field drawings are available. Distribution of data within the catalogue is as follows.

The extreme left sides of the left-hand pages show the Webb Society catalogue number (WS), these continuing in numerical sequence from the last entry in the catalogue of open clusters in Part Three. Each Webb Society number is followed by the actual designation of the cluster while for those clusters which are Messier objects the Messier number will appear below the relevant NGC number.

The remaining data, covering the greater parts of the left-hand pages, is as follows.

Upper Line.

(a) Positions for 1975.0

(b) V magnitudes of clusters (m), (Kukarkin 1974).

(c) Angular diameters of clusters in arcminutes (AD). All of the diameters are photographic measures (Alcaino 1973).

(d) Concentration classes of clusters (Con Cl), (Arp 1965).

(e) The abbreviated form of the relevant constellations (Con).

In a number of cases additional information will be found below the data displayed on the upper line.

Visual Observations.

The data below the dotted lines are contracted renderings of observations from the Webb Society files. The observations are set out in order of decreasing aperture, the figures in parenthesis, (40) (8) etc., are the respective apertures in inches. All quoted magnitudes, diameters etc. are purely eye estimates. Where observations made by more than one person using identical telescopes are concerned, the results have been run together into a single section.

Field Drawings.

These will be found on the opposite pages to the relevant observations, and consequently number four to a page. All the drawings are shown in circles of 57 mm diameter, regardless of the actual field diameters in arcminutes. Orientation is north down, east to the right.

A Catalogue of Globular Clusters.

List of Observers.

The following list shows the names of the observers whose work appears in the catalogue, plus details of their locations and respective telescopes.

D.A. Allen.	60-inch	Teneriffe, Canary Islands.
	40	Cerro las Campanas, Chile.
	12 o.g.	Cambridge, U.K.
	8½	" "
	8	" "
J. Perkins.	18	Chesterfield, U.K.
P. Andrew.	18	" "
M.J. Thomson.	16½	Santa Barbara, U.S.A.
S. Selleck.	10, 8, 6 o.g.	" " "
S.J. Hynes.	8½	Wistaston, U.K.
E.S. Barker.	8½	Herne Bay, "
C. Nugent.	8½	Pontefract, "
K. Glyn Jones.	8	Winkfield, "
K. Sturdy.	6	Helmsley, "
D. Branchett.	3.	Bishopstoke,"

Binoculars.
D.A. Allen.	7 x 35	
D. Branchett.	15 x 80, 20 x 50.	

Observers and Accredited Clusters.

The following list shows all the globular clusters that are featured in the first section of the catalogue (with field drawings) plus the initials of the respective observers. Clusters are listed in catalogue order, i.e., in order of RA.

NGC 1904 MJT, SS, KS.	NGC 6235 MJT, SS, DB.
2419 MJT, DAA, JP.	6254 MJT, SH, SS.
4147 MJT, DAA, SS, DB.	6266 KGJ, DB.
4590 KGJ, SS, KS, DB.	6273 DAA, KGJ, SS, DB.
5024 DAA, SS, KGJ, KS.	6284 SS, DB.
5053 MJT, DAA, SS, DB.	6287 SS, DB.
5272 MJT, SH, SS, KS.	6325 SS, DB.
5466 MJT, SS, DB.	6341 JP, PA, MJT, SH, KS.
5634 MJT, DAA, SS.	6333 DAA, SS, SH.
5897 MJT, SS.	6342 SS, DB.
5904 DAA, MJT, KGJ.	6356 DAA, SS, DB.
6093 DAA, SS, ESB, SS, DB.	6402 DAA, KGJ, KS.
6121 MJT, SS, SH, DB.	6401 SS, DB.
6144 MJT, DAA.	6426 SS, DB.
6171 DAA, SS, DB.	6517 SS, DB.
6205 JP, PA, DAA, SH, KGJ, KS, DB.	6535 MJT, SS, DB.
6218 MJT, DAA, KGJ, KS.	6539 SS.
6229 MJT, DAA, ESB, DB.	6626 MJT, SH, KGJ, SS, KS.

A Catalogue of Globular Clusters.

NGC 6638 MJT, SS.

    6637 SH, SS.

    6656 DAA, SH, KGJ, SS.

    6681 KGJ, SS, DB.

    6712 MJT, SS, KS.

    6715 KGJ, SS.

    6760 MJT, DAA.

    6779 MJT, KGJ, KS.

    6809 SH, KS.

NGC 6838 DAA, SH, KS.

    6864 DAA, KGJ.

    6934 MJT, SS, DB.

    6981 MJT, KGJ.

    7006 MJT, SH, KS.

    7078 DAA, MJT, KGJ.

    7089 SH, KGJ, KS.

    7099 CN, KGJ, KS, DB.

Below are shown the globular clusters for which no field drawings are available, and which form the second section of the catalogue. These include ω Cen, which although below the declination limit of this Handbook, is a striking object worthy of inclusion. The format is identical with the preceding list.

NGC 288 DAA.

   5139 DAA, MJT.

   5694 SS.

   6293 SS.

   6304 SS.

NGC 6316 SS.

   6355 SS.

   6366 SS.

   6440 MJT, SS.

   6642 MJT.

A Catalogue of Globular Clusters.

Part One : Descriptions and Field Drawings of 53 Globular Clusters.

WS	Cat	RA	Dec	m	AD	Con Cl	Con
367	NGC 1904	05 23.2	−24 33	7.84	7.8	V	Lep
	M79						

Brightest stars 14 mag.

- -

(16½) Extensive core; many bright members on f. side
at HP; easy to resolve.

(8) Outer areas resolved x241, more so to the N.

(6) Small, nebulous; bright, non-stellar centre.

| 368 | NGC 2419 | 07 36.5 | +38 57 | 10.80 | 6.2 | II | Lyn |

Very distant object; figures range from 61 to 83 kpc

- -

(16½) Irregularly round with bright centre; no sign
of resolution to x333, but cluster shows mottling.

(12) 2' diam.; faint and not well condensed.

(10) Faint haze with slightly brighter centre, the
latter showing signs of mottling x132.

| 369 | NGC 4147 | 12 08.9 | +18 41 | 10.28 | 4.1 | VI | Com |

- -

(16½) Bright nucleus; fades slightly at edges which
are just resolvable on MP.

(12) x80 2' diam.; fairly condensed.

(8) Brighter centre; star seen on N.p. edge.

(15 x 80) Very faint, small oval; elusive object.

| 370 | NGC 4590 | 12 38.1 | −26 37 | 8.5 | 9.8 | X | Hya |
| | M68 | | | | | | |

Stars 12 mag and below.

- -

(8) Round disc about 4' diam. with arcs of brighter
stars in the S and W regions; orange star about 5'
NW of centre; x296 well-resolved, but a haze of
unresolved stars still evident.

(6) 4' diam., unresolved; too low for HP.

(3) Faint, large oval haze; unresolved x40.

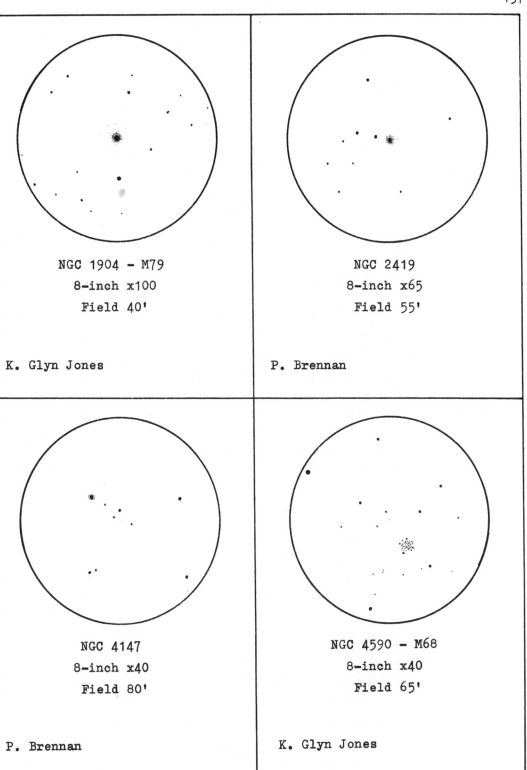

NGC 1904 — M79
8-inch x100
Field 40'

K. Glyn Jones

NGC 2419
8-inch x65
Field 55'

P. Brennan

NGC 4147
8-inch x40
Field 80'

P. Brennan

NGC 4590 — M68
8-inch x40
Field 65'

K. Glyn Jones

WS	Cat	RA	Dec	m	AD	Con Cl	Con
371	NGC 5024	13 11.7	+18 18	7.71	14.4	V	Com
	M53						

Brightest stars 13.8. Very old cluster.

- -

(12) Bright, weakly resolved; 3' diam.

(10) Very compressed; x148 edges resolved and stars quite scattered; x445 resolution at centre.

(8) Brilliant nucleus, about 2' diam., surrounded by a halo of light; takes moderate magnification.

(6) Fine object; partially resolved x120.

372	NGC 5053	13 15.1	+17 48	9.98	8.9	XI	Com

Low luminosity cluster; 3,400 stars to 21 mag.

- -

(16½) x70 diffuse spot with few stars resolved; still sparse but completely resolved x222, x333.

(12) x250 very difficult; 2' diam.

(10) Best at LP; a few stars seen at centre x296.

(15 x 80) Very faint, small oval.

373	NGC 5272	13 41.1	+28 30	6.41	18.6	VI	CVn
	M3						

Contains stars of 12.4 mag and below.

- -

(16½) Core resolved x222; p. side appears richer due possibly to dark bay in S.f. region.

(8½) Just resolved x154; bluish tinge suspected.

(8) Very compact and much brighter at the centre; x121 beautifully resolved almost to the middle.

(6) Granular at HP; centre not resolved.

374	NGC 5466	14 14.3	+28 39	9.35	9.2	XII	Boo

Contains stars of 15 mag and below.

- -

(16½) Lacks central concentration and is completely resolved x160; not rich in stars.

(8) Large but faint; some resolution x121; difficult.

(15 x 80) Faint, opaque cloud; easily overlooked.

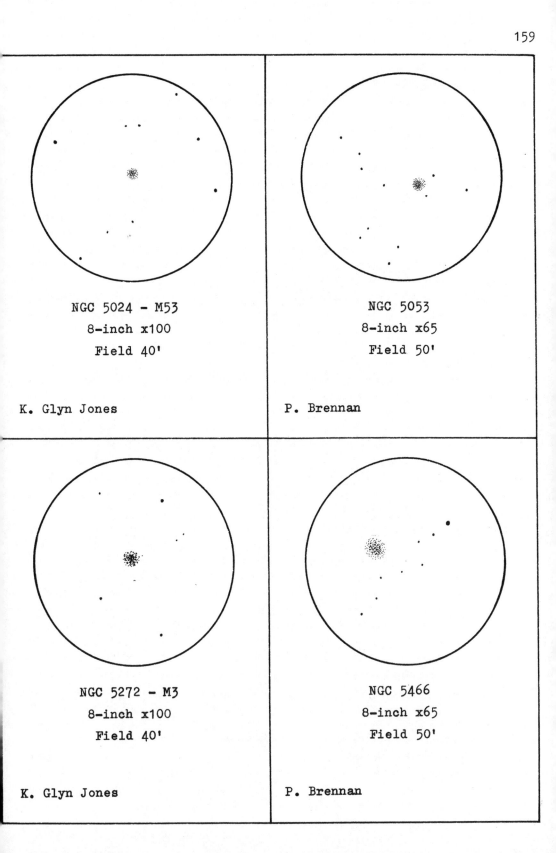

NGC 5024 – M53
8-inch x100
Field 40'

K. Glyn Jones

NGC 5053
8-inch x65
Field 50'

P. Brennan

NGC 5272 – M3
8-inch x100
Field 40'

K. Glyn Jones

NGC 5466
8-inch x65
Field 50'

P. Brennan

WS	Cat	RA	Dec	m	AD	Con Cl	Con
375	NGC 5634	14 28.3	−05 52	9.58	3.7	IV	Vir

(16½) Mottled x160; outer areas resolved x222.

(12) x250 barely resolved edges; not much condensed.

(10) x445 entire cluster mottled; very compact.

WS	Cat	RA	Dec	m	AD	Con Cl	Con
376	NGC 5897	15 15.9	−20 55	8.59	8.7	XI	Lib

(16½) Only slightly brighter in the middle; many faint stars visible x70; lacks any bright member.

(8) Pretty bright and large; some resolution x145.

WS	Cat	RA	Dec	m	AD	Con Cl	Con
377	NGC 5904 M5	15 17.3	+02 11	6.03	19.9	V	Ser

Contains stars of 12 mag and below.

(60) 12' diam.; loose object which is well-resolved almost to the middle.

(16½) Exceedingly bright; large central area with a bright star almost at centre; x70 outer ⅔ resolved and further magnification fills the field of view.

(8) Curves of separate stars to the N and little knots of stars to the S; magnifies well.

WS	Cat	RA	Dec	m	AD	Con Cl	Con
378	NGC 6093 M80	16 15.6	−22 56	7.31	5.1	II	Sco

Contains stars of 13.7 mag and below. 6.5 mag nova seen in 1860. Extensive nebulosity close by this cluster.

(12) 4' diam.; bright and well-condensed.

(10) Small, compact; outer parts resolved at MP.

(8½) Bright, almost stellar nucleus; stands high magnification well, but only shows mottled edges.

(6) x183 slight resolution at the edges and with x305 to x457 quite good resolution obtained.

(15 x 80) Just identifiable.

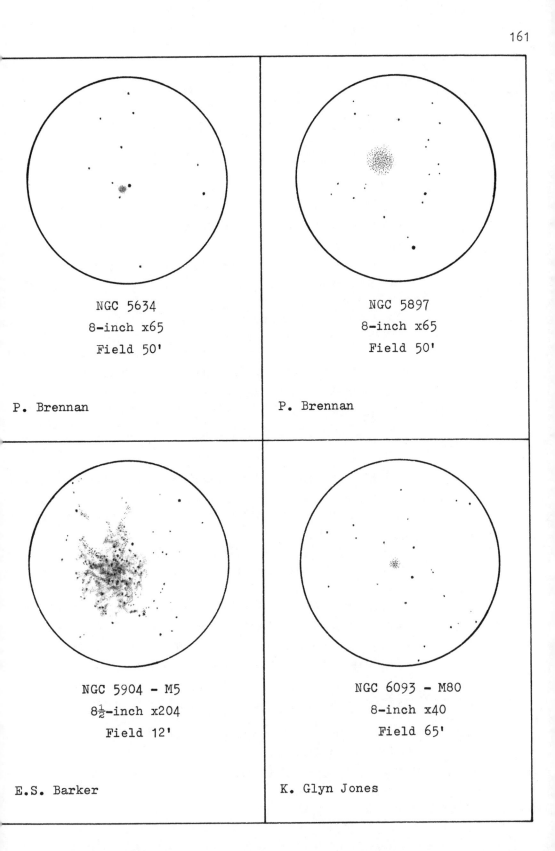

NGC 5634
8-inch x65
Field 50'

P. Brennan

NGC 5897
8-inch x65
Field 50'

P. Brennan

NGC 5904 — M5
8½-inch x204
Field 12'

E.S. Barker

NGC 6093 — M80
8-inch x40
Field 65'

K. Glyn Jones

WS	Cat	RA	Dec	m	AD	Con Cl	Con
379	NGC 6121	16 22.1	-26 27	5.96	22.8	IX	Sco
	M4						

Brightest stars 10.8 mag. In region of Antares moving cluster.

- -

(16½) Exceedingly rich with highly concentrated centre; resolves well at HP.

(10) Well-resolved at powers from x59 to x296; at the centre a line of stars N.f. – S.p.

(8½) Bright cluster stars lie in 2 converging bands, the N-S one containing at least 2 pairs.

(3) Stars scattered around the edges.

380	NGC 6144	16 25.7	-25 49	9.07	6.2	XI	Sco

- -

(16½) Mottled background with a few stars resolved.

(12) x80 1' diam.; very difficult object.

381	NGC 6171	16 31.1	-12 59	8.17	7.8	X	Oph
	M107						

(12) x80 3' diam.; unresolved.

(8) x145 resolved to the centre; suspected dark area.

(3) Faint, elusive opaque haze.

382	NGC 6205	16 40.8	+36 30	5.86	23.2	V	Her
	M13						

Brightest stars red giants of 12 mag. Over 30,000 star to 21 mag. Total number of stars about 1 million.

- -

(18) Wholly resolved with very crowded centre; many yellow stars, and three-dimensional effect very strong

(12) 10' diam.; several hundred stars resolved.

(8½) x154 cloud of tiny stars with brighter ones interspersed; nucleus about 4' diam.; no colours.

(8) Slightly flattened on E side; magnifies well and is resolvable practically to the centre.

(6) x130 fully resolved; lanes of stars from N to SE.

(10 x 50) Bright, compact nebular haze.

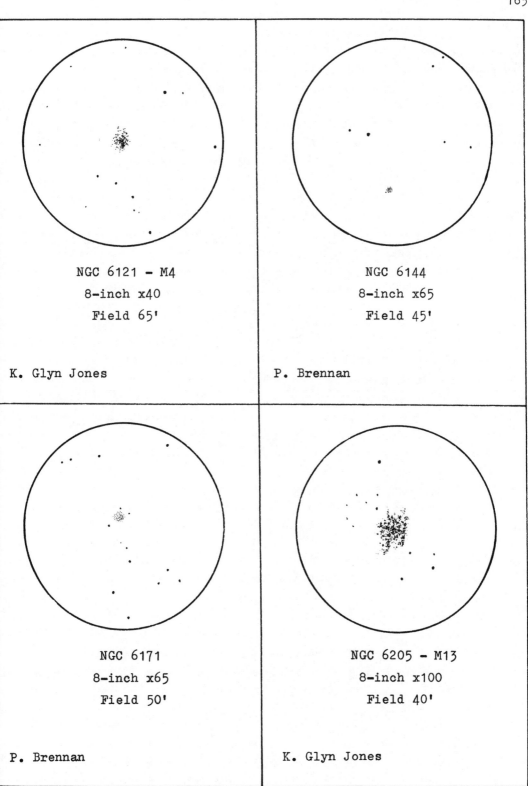

NGC 6121 - M4
8-inch x40
Field 65'

K. Glyn Jones

NGC 6144
8-inch x65
Field 45'

P. Brennan

NGC 6171
8-inch x65
Field 50'

P. Brennan

NGC 6205 - M13
8-inch x100
Field 40'

K. Glyn Jones

WS	Cat	RA	Dec	m	AD	Con Cl	Con
383	NGC 6218	16 45.9	-01 55	6.88	12.2	IX	Oph
	M12						

Contains stars of 11 mag and below.

- -

(16½) Core large and very bright; x70 outer areas resolved into many small stars.

(12) 5' diam.; just resolved at the edges.

(8) Easily resolved; outline far from circular and the slightly denser centre flattened to the SW.

(6) Partly resolved; two short lanes on p. side.

384	NGC 6229	16 46.3	+47 34	9.39	3.8	IV	Her

- -

(16½) Bright, small and round; central area almost stellar x70; not easily resolved, x333 showing it to be mottled with just a few faint stars visible.

(12) x80 faint and unresolved; 2' diam.

(20 x 50) Faint, small oval blob.

385	NGC 6235	16 51.9	-22 07	10.4	1.9	IV	Oph

- -

(16½) Small, pretty bright; no resolution.

(10) Faint, slightly brighter towards the centre at x59; x296 slight resolution.

(3) Very faint, small and difficult.

386	NGC 6254	16 55.8	-04 04	6.63	12.2	VII	Oph
	M10						

Brightest stars 11.6 mag. No RR Lyrae stars and few other variables are in this cluster.

- -

(16½) Very bright core; x70 numerous stars on the edges and x160 a large number of bright stars in the centre; x222 dark starless regions on the S edge of centre.

(8½) 10' diam.; central 4' nebulous at LP; a number of stars resolved x77 and well-resolved x154.

(6) x457 resolved in centre; compact and even at LP.

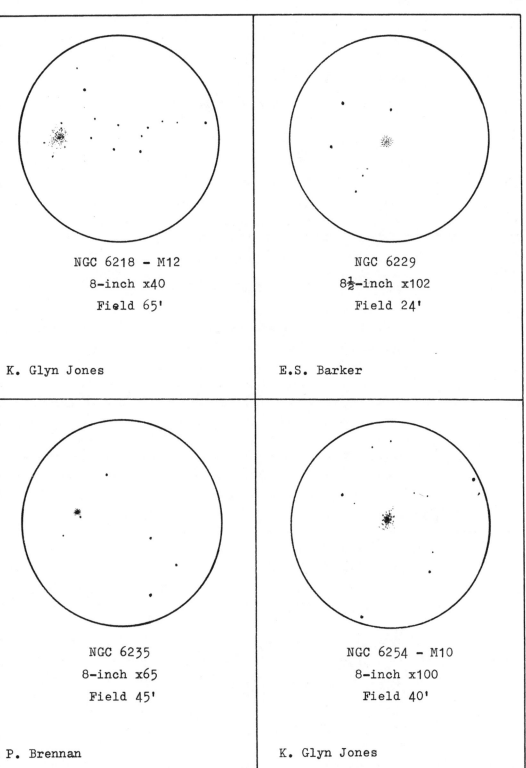

NGC 6218 — M12
8-inch x40
Field 65'

K. Glyn Jones

NGC 6229
8½-inch x102
Field 24'

E.S. Barker

NGC 6235
8-inch x65
Field 45'

P. Brennan

NGC 6254 — M10
8-inch x100
Field 40'

K. Glyn Jones

WS	Cat	RA	Dec	m	AD	Con Cl	Con
387	NGC 6266	16 59.7	-30 05	6.53	6.3	IV	Sco
	M62						

The SE region of this cluster is obscured by a dust cloud (A_V = 0.75 mag) relative to the NW region.

- -

(8) Small, very bright with a slight bluish glow; mos condensed portion to SE of centre with stars fanning out to the NW, giving a comet-like look; moderate magnification resolves all but the SE part.

(3) Bright, fans out in all directions.

388	NGC 6273	17 01.0	-26 13	6.83	5.3	VIII	Oph
	M19						

- -

(12) 4' diam.; elongated N-S; edges barely resolved.

(8) Edges fairly easily resolved on MP; about 10 to 15% longer N-S than E-W; x241 very well resolved with edges quite straggling; does not stand use of high powers from mid-northern latitudes.

(3) Very bright oval with stars scattered on edges.

389	NGC 6284	17 03.0	-24 43	9.03	2.7	IX	Oph

- -

(10) x59 quite compact, spherical and brighter toward the centre; edges ill-defined. x148 slightly resolved and well-resolved at x445.

(3) Bright oval with edges fanning out.

390	NGC 6287	17 03.6	-22 40	9.44	2.7	VII	Oph

Brightest stars 15.4 mag. This cluster lies in a regi of dark nebulosity connected with the Antares moving cluster. Absorption is over 2 magnitudes.

- -

(10) Pretty bright, compact and spherical x59; x148 and x296 suspected resolution around edges.

(3) Bright oval nebulosity.

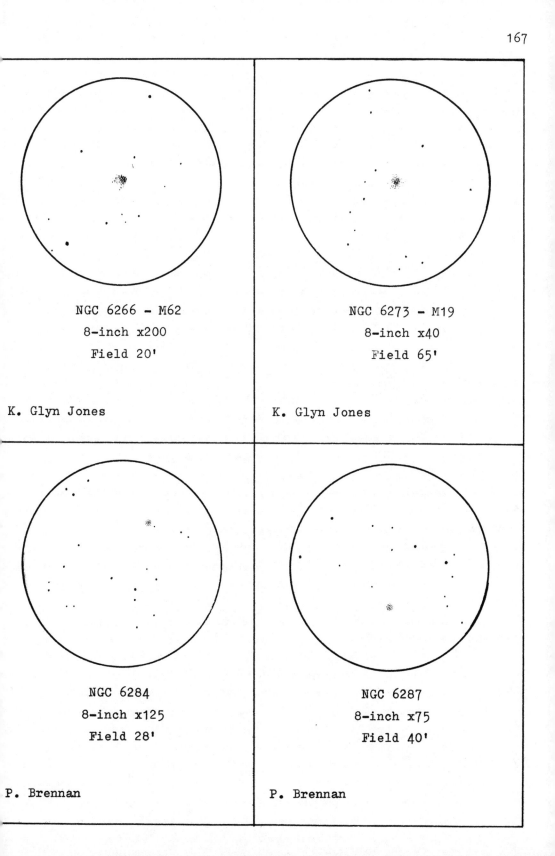

NGC 6266 — M62
8-inch x200
Field 20'

K. Glyn Jones

NGC 6273 — M19
8-inch x40
Field 65'

K. Glyn Jones

NGC 6284
8-inch x125
Field 28'

P. Brennan

NGC 6287
8-inch x75
Field 40'

P. Brennan

WS	Cat	RA	Dec	m	AD	Con Cl	Con
391	NGC 6325	17 16.5	−23 44	10.73	1.6	X	Oph

(10) x59 faint and slightly brighter towards the centre with ill-defined edges; x148 and x296 slight traces of resolution.

(3) Very faint and small; elusive object.

392	NGC 6341	17 16.4	+43 10	6.50	12.2	IV	Her
	M92						

(18) Total resolution with the centre a knotty mass of stars with overlaying brighter ones; The N.edge much flatter than the irregularity of the rest.

(16½) Exceedingly bright central region with the E edge richer in faint stars; x222 dark areas on the E side between the core and a line of stars; between lines of stars running SW to E is a larger dark area.

(8½) x77 resolved around periphery; x154 2' nucleus at the centre of a swarm of stars of 12 mag and below several stars resolved in the nucleus.

(6) Bright nucleus and many outliers; f. side fainter

393	NGC 6333	17 17.7	−18 30	7.75	5.5	VIII	Oph
	M9						

The brightest stars in this cluster about 13.1 mag.

(12) x80 5' diam., quite bright, moderately condensed

(10) Very compressed x59; beautifully resolved x445.

(8½) About 7' diam.; outer areas resolved on MP.

394	NGC 6342	17 19.7	−19 33	10.10	1.3	IV	Oph

(10) x59 small, fairly bright and uniform; x296 is slightly resolved and possibly not circular.

(3) Faint but easily seen on clear nights.

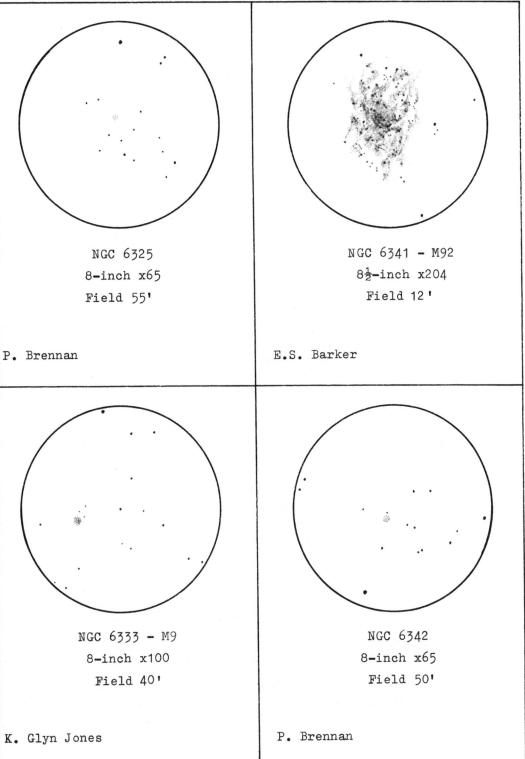

NGC 6325
8-inch x65
Field 55'

P. Brennan

NGC 6341 – M92
8½-inch x204
Field 12'

E.S. Barker

NGC 6333 – M9
8-inch x100
Field 40'

K. Glyn Jones

NGC 6342
8-inch x65
Field 50'

P. Brennan

WS	Cat	RA	Dec	m	AD	Con Cl	Con
395	NGC 6356	17 22.2	-17 47	8.28	3.5	II	Oph

(12) x80 2' diam., uniform brightness.

(10) x59 compact and spherical with ill-defined edges; x296 resolution of outer stars.

(3) Bright, opaque cloud.

396	NGC 6402	17 36.3	-03 16	7.49	6.7	VIII	Oph
	M14						

Stars of 15.6 mag and below. A nova of 16 mag appeared in this cluster in 1964, but may not have been a membe

(12) x80 2'.5 diam., quite bright, moderately condense

(8) Seems fainter than given mag; perfectly round, haz patch showing trace of resolution at the periphery wit x100; no definite central condensation.

(6) Nebulous glow partly resolved; very slight hint of nucleus; diam about 4'.

397	NGC 6401	17 37.1	-23 54	9.44	1.0	?	Oph

This cluster obscured by about 2.69 mag.

(10) x59 quite compact and spherical with edges not we defined; x148 one or two stars seen towards the centre x296 dark areas suspected.

(3) Small, bright oval

398	NGC 6426	17 43.6	+03 11	11.48	2.2	IX	Oph

This cluster obscured by a little over 0.75 mag.

(8) x48 faint and circular with very gradual central brightening; x121 appears to be mottled and the border are irregular. x145, x241 a few stars noticeable.

(3) Faint, small elusive object.

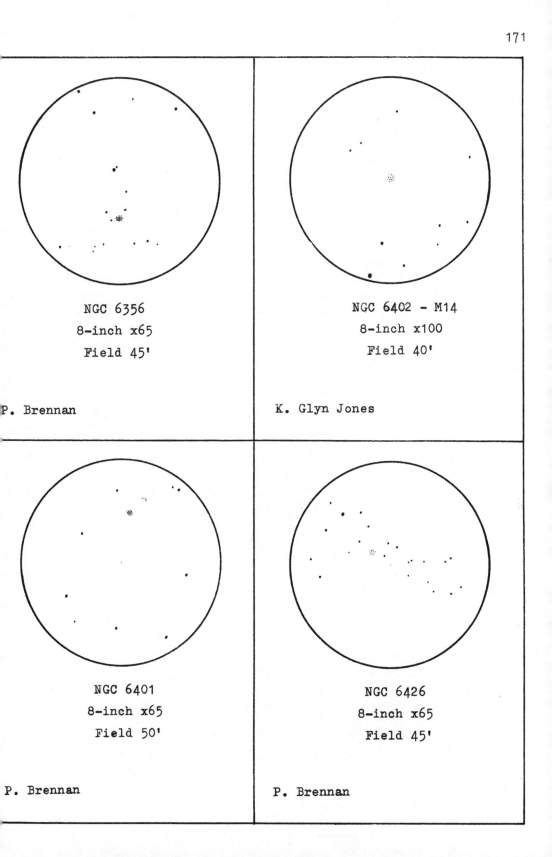

NGC 6356
8-inch x65
Field 45'

P. Brennan

NGC 6402 - M14
8-inch x100
Field 40'

K. Glyn Jones

NGC 6401
8-inch x65
Field 50'

P. Brennan

NGC 6426
8-inch x65
Field 45'

P. Brennan

WS	Cat	RA	Dec	m	AD	Con Cl	Con
399	NGC 6517	18 00.5	-08 57	10.29	1.0	IV	Oph

(10) Faint and small x59 with very gradual brighteni
towards the centre; x445 some resolution obtained bu
this is difficult to achieve.
(3) Very faint and small; difficult.

| 400 | NGC 6535 | 18 02.6 | -00 18 | 10.62 | 1.3 | XI | Oph |

(16½) Small and faint x70 with irregularly round sha
a few stars resolved around the edges, the four
brightest being on the W edge.
(6) x152 slight resolution; possible star on the S.p.
edge; becomes difficult with increasing magnification
(3) Faint, elusive object.

| 401 | NGC 6539 | 18 03.5 | -07 35 | 9.62 | 3.5 | X | Ser |

(10) Uniform in brightness and appears on the verge o
resolution x59; x296 slight resolution to the extent
of about five fairly bright stars on the edges.

| 402 | NGC 6626 | 18 23.0 | -24 53 | 6.99 | 15.0 | IV | Sgr |
| | M28 | Brightest stars in this cluster about 13.2 mag. | | | | | |

(16½) Easily resolved x84; bright, irregularly round
centre with outer parts consisting of a large number
of small stars; fine sight x176.
(8½) Small, circular nebulosity x56; not resolved x11
but suspicion of peripheral resolution x155.
(8) Compact object with bright, glowing centre which
fades off rapidly towards the edges. At mid-northern
latitudes it appears smaller and fainter than
expected, and only resolves at the edges with some
difficulty; from California x241 resolves totally.
(6) 2' - 3' diam.; bright, stellar centre.

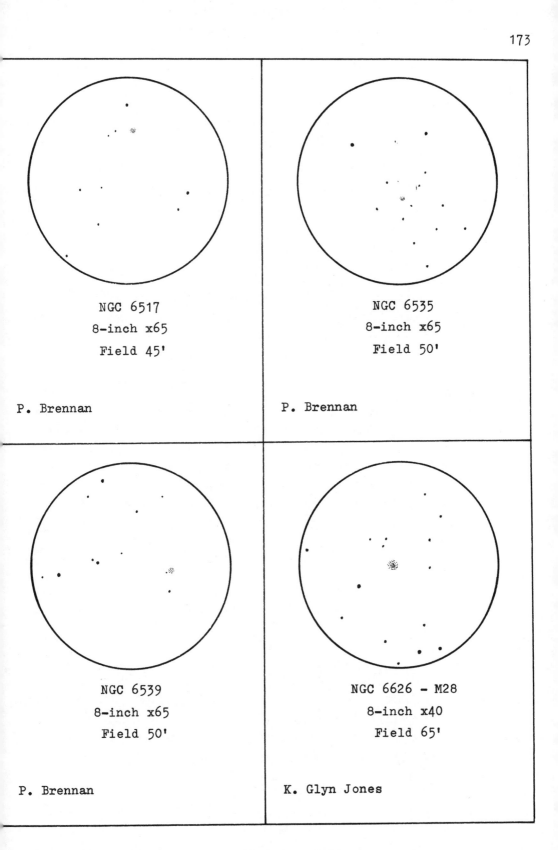

NGC 6517
8-inch x65
Field 45'

P. Brennan

NGC 6535
8-inch x65
Field 50'

P. Brennan

NGC 6539
8-inch x65
Field 50'

P. Brennan

NGC 6626 – M28
8-inch x40
Field 65'

K. Glyn Jones

WS	Cat	RA	Dec	m	AD	Con Cl	Con
403	NGC 6638	18 29.4	-25 31	9.03	2.2	VI	Sgr

(16½) x351 well-resolved, the majority of stars being on the NE edge.

(8) Small, bright with a few outer members resolved.

| 404 | NGC 6637 M69 | 18 29.7 | -32 22 | 7.79 | 3.8 | V | Sgr |

The brightest stars in this cluster are 13.2 mag.

(8½) Fairly bright and small, with outer regions a little irregular; hardly any central condensation, and x250 resolved the cluster into faint, evenly-spaced stars; difficult from mid-northern latitudes.

(6) x305 resolved to the centre.

| 405 | NGC 6656 M22 | 18 34.8 | -23 57 | 5.07 | 17.0 | VII | Sgr |

The brightest stars in this cluster are of 11 mag, including one reddish object. There is obscuring material in the region absorbing by 1.72 magnitudes.

(12) Well-resolved; very large and bright.

(8½) Already resolved x56; elongated E-W with well-spaced stars, including brighter one on S edge; diam. 10'.

(8) Fine, large object easily resolvable to the centre distinctly non-circular.

(6) x152 cluster covers the entire field; contains a knot of stars situated N of centre.

| 406 | NGC 6681 M70 | 18 41.6 | -32 20 | 8.18 | 4.1 | V | Sgr |

(8) Small with sharp central condensation around which is a fainter area seemingly slightly flattened to the E; outer edges resolved x250.

(6) Bright centre; edges resolved x152, x183.

(3) Very bright nebulous cloud.

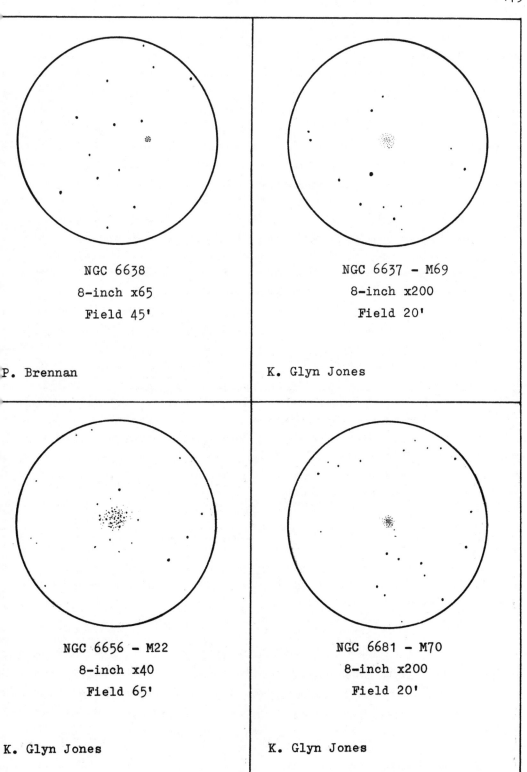

NGC 6638
8-inch x65
Field 45'

P. Brennan

NGC 6637 – M69
8-inch x200
Field 20'

K. Glyn Jones

NGC 6656 – M22
8-inch x40
Field 65'

K. Glyn Jones

NGC 6681 – M70
8-inch x200
Field 20'

K. Glyn Jones

WS	Cat	RA	Dec	m	AD	Con Cl	Con
407	NGC 6712	18 51.7	-08 45	8.13	4.2	IX	Sct

The brightest stars in this cluster are 13.3 mag.

- -

(16½) Easily resolved at LP; at HP a definite dark lane between the centre and the SE edge; irregular.
(8) Easily resolved x121; x241 possible dark areas.
(6) Moderately condensed and easily resolved.

408	NGC 6715	18 53.6	-30 30	7.61	5.5	III	Sgr
	M54						

The brightest stars in this cluster are 15.6 mag.

- -

(8) Very small and bright, almost like a planetary nebula at first sight; stands HP well, but from mid-northern latitudes even x250 fails to resolve; from southern California the halo of outer stars is very slightly resolved and the cluster is slightly extended E-W; one brighter star on S edge.

409	NGC 6760	19 09.9	+00 59	9.08	2.4	IX	Aql

- -

(16½) Outer edges mottled x84; x176 brightens very gradually towards the middle while outer edges are still diffuse; x351 bright knot towards S edge, but no actual resolution obtained.
(12) 1' diam., unresolved.

410	NGC 6779	19 15.6	+30 08	8.21	2.4	X	Lyr
	M56						

The brightest stars in this cluster are 13.1 mag.

- -

(16½) Non-circular shape; resolves completely to the centre and contains a bright star near NW edge of co:
(8) Small, moderately bright and of even density witl no very marked central condensation; central region (about 4' diam. gives a slightly three-lobed impressi(too faint to take high magnification for resolution.
(6) Irregular outline; partial resolution x120.

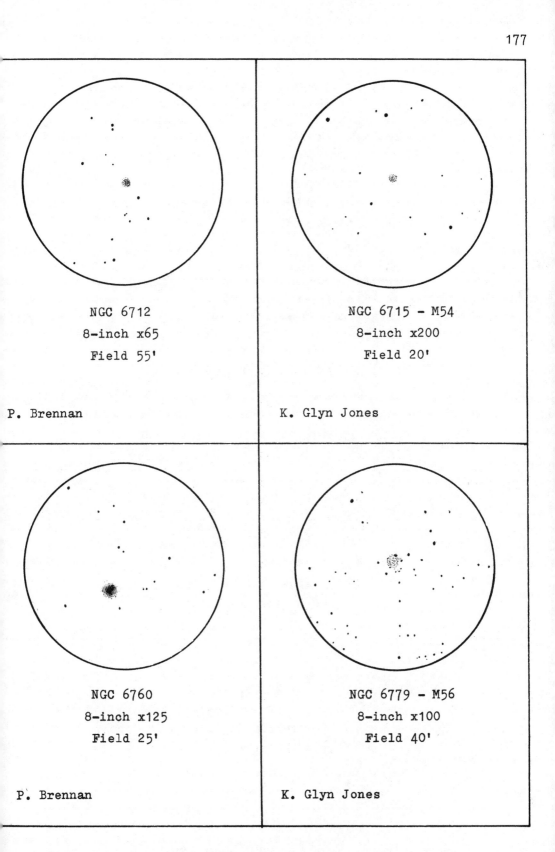

NGC 6712
8-inch x65
Field 55'

P. Brennan

NGC 6715 – M54
8-inch x200
Field 20'

K. Glyn Jones

NGC 6760
8-inch x125
Field 25'

P. Brennan

NGC 6779 – M56
8-inch x100
Field 40'

K. Glyn Jones

WS	Cat	RA	Dec	m	AD	Con Cl	Con
411	NGC 6809	19 38.5	-31 00	6.33	14.8	XI	Sgr
	M55						

The brightest stars in this cluster are 11.2 mag.

- -

(8½) Very difficult to see from mid-northern regions; however, it is large, and can be resolved on MP; on HP elongated N-S with an irregular outline; stars of about 12 mag and below.

(6) Resolved to the centre x68; contains quite a few chains of stars.

412	NGC 6838	19 52.6	+18 43	8.28	6.1	?	Sge
	M71						

The brightest stars in this cluster are 12.0 mag. An Algol-type eclipsing variable is a member.

- -

(12) x80 4' diam., just resolved.

(8½) Low surface brightness and no indication of a nucleus; certain degree of granularity with a few sta possibly resolved; poor image at HP.

(6) Nebulosity concentrated in W oart.

413	NGC 6864	20 04.7	-22 00	8.52	4.6	I	Sgr
	M75						

The brightest stars in this cluster are 15.6 mag.

- -

(12) x80 2' diam., bright but unresolved.

(8) Compact, about 2' - 3' diam. with bright centre o about 1' in size; x120 a slight mottling of the edges seen; higher powers not satisfactory from a latitude of 51½° N.

414	NGC 6934	20 32.9	+07 19	9.03	6.2	VIII	Del

- -

(16½) x70 mottled, especially on the S side, and this and the E edge resolved at x160; at HP the W side shows negligable resolution, unlike the rest.

(8) Partial resolution to x362.

(15 x 80) Faint, small oval disc.

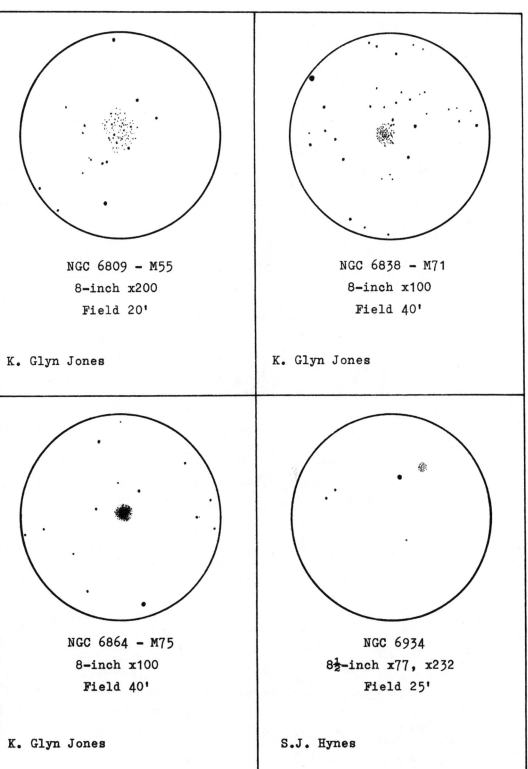

NGC 6809 - M55
8-inch x200
Field 20'

K. Glyn Jones

NGC 6838 - M71
8-inch x100
Field 40'

K. Glyn Jones

NGC 6864 - M75
8-inch x100
Field 40'

K. Glyn Jones

NGC 6934
$8\frac{1}{2}$-inch x77, x232
Field 25'

S.J. Hynes

WS	Cat	RA	Dec	m	AD	Con Cl	Con
415	NGC 6981 M72	20 52.1	−12 38	9.35	5.1	IX	Aqr

(16½) Easily resolved on the outer edges x70; x160 and x222 an area of resolved stars on the NE side see almost separated by a dark region.
(8) Even brightness and difficult to resolve with a moderate aperture owing to its faintness.

416	NGC 7006	21 00.3	+16 06	10.67	2.2	I	Del

The brightest stars in this cluster are 16.0 mag. Thi is possibly an intergalactic object like NGC 2419.

(16½) x84 bright centre surrounded by a nebulous shel x176 irregularly round with inner and outer parts showing ill-defined edges; not resolved.
(8½) x222 momentary glimpses of mottling at the centr
(6) Small with diffuse nucleus; very ill-defined.

417	NGC 7078 M15	21 28.8	+12 04	6.48	12.3	IV	Peg

Contains the 13.8 mag planetary nebula Ps 1, situated about 30" NW of centre. Diam. of the nebula 1".

(40) Very impressive; resolved almost to the centre.
(16½) Extremely bright core x70; x333 completely fill the field; easily resolvable.
(8) Large area of resolvable stars around centre; tot size not less than 8'.

418	NGC 7089 M2	21 32.2	−00 56	6.50	11.7	II	Aqr

The brightest stars in this cluster are 13.2 mag.

(8½) About 5' diam., uniformly bright nucleus with several faint stars resolved on the edges.
(8) Takes MP well; outer edges resolved and at times a greenish-blue glow surrounds the cluster.
(6) Very condensed; outer areas resolved x120.

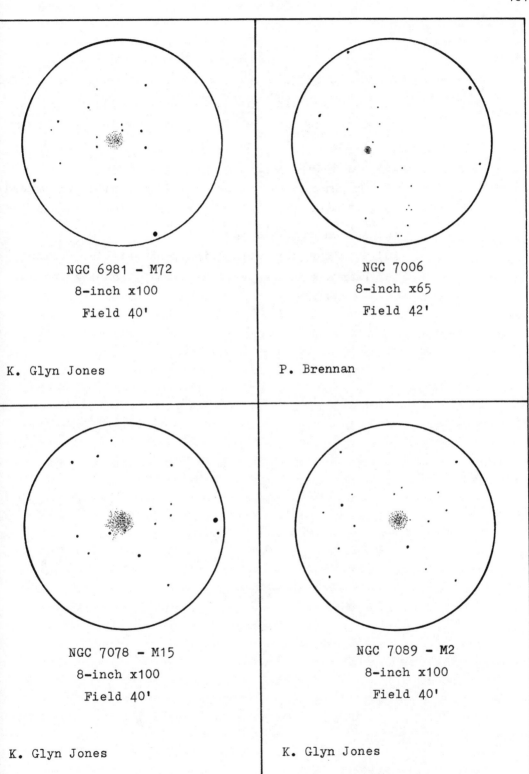

NGC 6981 — M72
8-inch x100
Field 40'

K. Glyn Jones

NGC 7006
8-inch x65
Field 42'

P. Brennan

NGC 7078 — M15
8-inch x100
Field 40'

K. Glyn Jones

NGC 7089 — M2
8-inch x100
Field 40'

K. Glyn Jones

WS	Cat	RA	Dec	m	AD	Con Cl	Con
419	NGC 7099	21 38.9	−23 18	7.56	8.9	V	Cap
	M30						

(8½) x56 granular but not resolved; x111 partially resolved including a line of stars extending N from the centre; x222 extensive resolution, but not in any way total.

(8) Bright nucleus about 1' − 2' diameter surrounded by a glowing area out to 5'; the centre is dense but resolution of the outer parts is easy.

(6) Nebulous glow with bright, non-stellar nucleus.

(3) Faint, elusive; extends evenly from the centre.

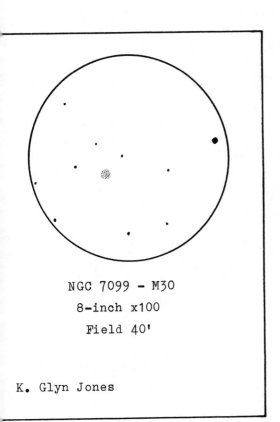

NGC 7099 - M30
8-inch x100
Field 40'

K. Glyn Jones

A Catalogue of Globular Clusters.

Part Two : Descriptions of a Further 10 Globular Clusters.

WS	Cat	RA	Dec	m	AD	Con Cl	Con
420	NGC 288	00 51.4	-26 44	8.56	12.4	X	Scl

(40) 10' diam.; beautiful object clearly resolved.

421	NGC 5139	13 25.3	-47 11	3.65	65.4	VIII	Cen
	ω Cen						

(40) Entire field covered with golden-red stars and
successive fields show no thinning of the stars for
a good number of moves in RA; about 3000 stars seen.
(16½) An unbelievable sight; x84 resolved to the
centre; no central core seen, just countless stars;
x176 more than fills the field, and a number of dark
areas are visible while numerous small groups of
stars appear to curve across the cluster; behind all
this is a diffuse nebulosity due to the effect of
thousands of unresolved stars.

422	NGC 5694	14 38.2	-26 25	10.17	2.2	VII	Hya

(10) x59 small and fairly bright, more so towards the
centre which is very compact; x148 the edges appear t
be on the verge of resolution and at x445 the cluster
resolves well.

423	NGC 6293	17 08.7	-26 32	8.79	3.5	IV	Oph

(10) x59 a very compact core and a halo of partially
resolved stars; resolved x445, and appears slightly
extended E-W; brighter star near the E edge.

424	NGC 6304	17 13.0	-29 26	8.38	3.8	VI	Oph

(8) Compact and spherical; resolution at x241.

425	NGC 6316	17 15.0	-28 07	9.00	2.4	III	Oph

(10) x59 pretty bright, a little more so towards the
centre; x296 resolution and some scattering seen.

WS	Cat	RA	Dec	m	AD	Con Cl	Con
126	NGC 6355	17 22.5	−26 19	9.76	1.0		Oph

(10) Quite compact; slight resolution at x296.

127	NGC 6366	17 26.4	−05 03	10.09	5.8	XI	Oph

(8) x145 beautifully resolved throughout although a haze of unresolved stars still evident.

128	NGC 6440	17 47.4	−20 21	9.39	1.7	V	Sgr

(16½) Small, with bright core surrounded by a halo of nebulosity; no resolution to x222.
(10) Compact object; slight resolution at x296.

129	NGC 6642	18 29.9	−23 29	8.8	0.8		Sgr

(16½) Small, quite bright with a small central core; at x176 very mottled at the edges with a few stars resolved, especially on the S edge; more resolution on the edges x351, the centre remaining bright.

LIST OF ADDITIONAL OBJECTS.

Cluster	RA	Dec	m	AD	Con Cl	Con
NGC 6558	18 08.6	−31 47				Sgr

This cluster is obscured by almost 2.5 magnitudes.

Cluster	RA	Dec	m	AD	Con Cl	Con
IC 1276	18 09.4	−07 14		6.0	XII	Ser
NGC 6717	18 53.6	−22 49		2.6	VIII	Sgr
NGC 6749	19 03.9	+01 44	11.7			Aql

This cluster is obscured by almost 7 magnitudes.

The following three clusters are members of the Fornax dwarf galaxy (E3 (d)), a member of the Local Group of galaxies. There are two other globular clusters associated with this galaxy, but these are much fainter objects.

Cluster	RA	Dec	m	AD	Con Cl	Con
NGC 1049	02 38.8	−34 41	11.0	0.6	V	For

The brightest cluster in the Fornax system, this object can act as a locus for identification of the remaining two clusters, whose positions relative to NGC 1049 are shown below.

Anon   Positioned 35' in PA 203° from NGC 1049.

Anon   Positioned 17' in PA 165° from the first Anon cluster. An 8 mag star lies about 7' p.

_APPENDIX 1.

CLASS 7 OPEN CLUSTERS.

In the Revised New General Catalogue (Sulentic and Tifft, 1973) Class 7 objects are defined as those whose images are not apparent on the Palomar Sky Survey prints. There are many true objects on these prints which are rendered virtually invisible due to heavy contamination by field stars or extensive and intense regions of emission nebulosity. We have examined numerous open clusters on the Sky Survey prints, and many are very heavily swamped by field stars on both the E and O-prints. A couple of examples are NGC 6800 and NGC 6815, the latter being located in an extremely rich field, and not appearing cluster-like at all.

Distributed over the sky are to be found many asterisms of stars; to all intents and purposes they appear like rather sparse open clusters, and a number have even found their way into Norton's Star Atlas. Some of these are described in the following pages, while others are: NGC 2318, NGC 2394, NGC 2413 and NGC 2430. Others, not charted in Norton's are: NGC 1524, NGC 6839, NGC 6856, NGC 6904.

Visual observers are able to isolate these asterisms with ease, as the faint stars surrounding them in such large numbers are well beyond the light-gathering abilities of moderate telescopes. In the following pages are to be found observations of 24 asterisms; as these are not true clusters, the only available data for them are their positions, which are shown for 1975.0. The observations have been made by Guy Hurst (10-inch) and Patrick Brennan (6-inch).

Appendix 1.

Cluster	RA	Dec		Con
NGC 358	01 03.6	+61 54		Cas

(10) In the same LP field as NGC 366; 4 stars in a
sparse field; could be nothing but an asterism.

NGC 2026	05 41.7	+20 06	Tau

(6) About 10' x 7' in size, showing a N-S elongation;
35 stars from 9 mag down; fainter stars in clumps.

NGC 2165	06 09.0	+51 41	Aur

(6) Coarse, but bright; an irregularly-shaped group of
about 6' diameter; 15 stars of 10 mag and below.

NGC 2184	06 09.7	-03 30	Ori

(6) Contains 35 stars of 9 mag and below distributed
evenly across a 15' field.

NGC 2234	06 28.0	+16 42	Gem

Plotted in Norton's Star Atlas.

(6) Irregular shape; contains about 40 stars of 11 mag
and below, unevenly distributed; 25' diameter.

NGC 2260	06 36.8	-01 27	Mon

Plotted in Norton's Star Atlas.

(6) About 50 stars of 8 mag and below scattered over
a 20' area; roundish in shape.

NGC 2306	06 53.4	-07 19	Mon

(10) Large triangle of three 8 mag stars enclosing
fainter ones; a 12 mag double lies at the centre and a
a very close 10 mag double on the S edge; doubtful
if it is a true cluster; 20' diameter; 27 stars.

Appendix 1.

Cluster	RA	Dec	Con
NGC 2356	07 15.8	+14 01	Gem

(10) At LP shows as a nebulous 7 mag star, and at HP
three 11 mag stars form a triangle close to the
7 mag; fainter stars possible within the 11 mag ones.

NGC 6561	18 19.1	−16 48	Sgr

Plotted in Norton's Star Atlas.

(6) Rather poor; contains stars of 9 to 11 mag, and
includes a triple of mags 9:9:12.

NGC 6832	19 47.7	+59 21	Cyg

(10) Not rich, and very like an asterism; centred on
a yellow 7 mag star with some evidence of fainter
stars nearby; scattered stars of 8 to 12 mag.

NGC 6840	19 54.1	+12 02	Aql

(6) About 5' diameter, containing 20 stars of 10 mag
and below; a similar but slightly poorer group,
NGC 6843, lies $\frac{1}{4}^{\circ}$ to the E.

NGC 6874	20 06.9	+38 10	Cyg

(10) Rich group with considerable haze; shows a
triangular-shaped outline and a 10 mag star on the
E edge displays an orange tint; 19 stars in 7' area.

NGC 6896	20 17.1	+30 33	Cyg

(10) Two slight condensations of star groups in a
rich field; both seem very like asterisms.

NGC 6989	20 53.2	+45 11	Cyg

(10) Quite large and faint; two faint doubles near
the centre; 10' diameter; 17 stars.

Appendix 1.

Cluster	RA	Dec	Con
NGC 6997	20 55.2	+44 33	Cyg

(10) Fairly large but faint; quite rich in certain areas with much haze; contains several faint doubles; 12' diameter; 28 stars.

NGC 7024	21 05.1	+41 24	Cyg

(10) Rich clustering of faint stars at the centre; a small, faint cluster grouped around a 10 mag star; 10' diameter; 14 stars.

NGC 7037	21 09.7	+33 37	Cyg

(10) Rich but difficult as the majority of stars are below 12 mag; 7' diameter; 10 stars.

NGC 7050	21 14.3	+36 05	Cyg

(10) A very poor group containing two small asterisms; stars scattered and faint.

NGC 7071	21 25.6	+47 49	Cyg

(10) Very small and difficult; x120 a small, misty patch of stars from 12 mag downwards; 4' diameter.

NGC 7175	21 57.9	+54 42	Cyg

(10) Triangular-shaped group with no bright stars; rather sparse; 8' diameter; 11 stars.

NGC 7234	22 11.2	+56 51	Cep

(10) Extremely faint, showing as a 13 mag double set in nebulosity; not seen at LP; 40" diameter.

NGC 7295	22 27.4	+52 42	Lac

(10) Small, faint; a 10 mag star with others of 11 to 12 mag; about 1' diameter.

Appendix 1.

Cluster	RA	Dec		Con
NGC 7352	22 38.7	+57 16		Cep

(10) Faint stars involved in some haze; requires HP to pick out faint stars in a 5' area.

NGC 7394	22 49.5	+52 02		Lac

(10) Between two 7 mag stars; faint and rather sparse; 19 stars between 11 and 12 mag; 11' diameter.

NGC 7795	23 57.4	+59 52		Cas

(10) Faint, scattered group; a yellow 7 mag star is near the centre, and the other stars are from 10 to 12 mag; 16' diameter; 17 stars.

APPENDIX 2.

FURTHER OBSERVATIONS OF OPEN CLUSTERS.

The observations depicted on pages 198 and 199 were received after the main catalogue had been compiled. The observations were made by Guy Hurst and Patrick Brennan, and as written descriptions were not made for all of the clusters, we show below just positions for 1975, magnitudes and angular diameters except for Cr 432, for which no data is available barring RA and Dec.

Guy Hurst: 10-inch spec.

Cluster	RA	Dec	m	AD
NGC 6996	$20^h\ 55^m.6$	$+44^\circ\ 32'$	10.1	9.0
Cr 428	21 02.3	+44 29	8.5	14.0
Cr 432	21 11.3	+47 38		

Patrick Brennan: 8-inch spec, 6-inch spec.

Cluster	RA	Dec	m	AD
NGC 2489	$07^h\ 55^m.2$	$-30^\circ\ 00'$	9.2	8.5
NGC 6631	18 25.8	-12 04	11.5	4.0
NGC 7762	23 48.6	+67 53	10.0	11.5

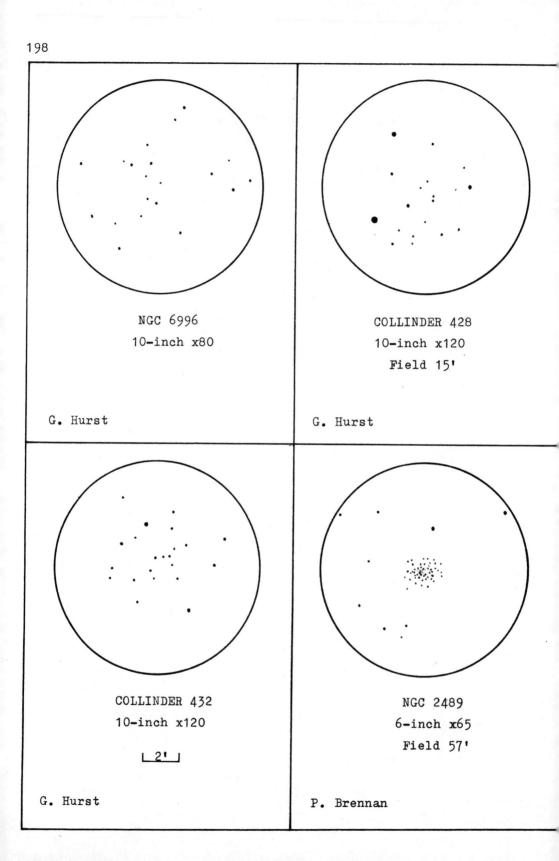

NGC 6996

10-inch x80

G. Hurst

COLLINDER 428

10-inch x120

Field 15'

G. Hurst

COLLINDER 432

10-inch x120

⌐ 2' ⌐

G. Hurst

NGC 2489

6-inch x65

Field 57'

P. Brennan

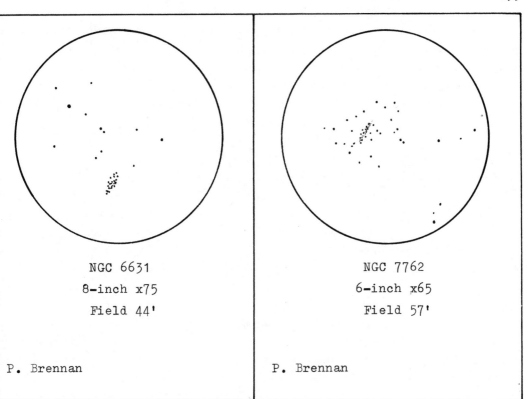

NGC 6631
8-inch x75
Field 44'

NGC 7762
6-inch x65
Field 57'

P. Brennan

P. Brennan

APPENDIX 3.

THE DISTANCES OF CLUSTERS.

In the chapters on the properties of open and globular clusters we dwelt briefly upon cluster ages, and we now introduce these once again, the reason being that the age of a cluster, and its distance, are determined simultaneously. In chapters 2 and 5 we saw that stars spend most of their lives on the main-sequence. The primary property of a main-sequence star is its mass, the most massive stars weigh one hundred times as much as the Sun, the least massive only a few times as much as Jupiter.

Once the mass is known, all other properties follow, including diameter, luminosity, surface temperature and life expectancy. A star's temperature is measured by spectroscopy, this being the easiest parameter to observe, and this in turn determines the star's luminosity, provided we know that the star is a main-sequence object. From the star's luminosity and apparent magnitude we can deduce its distance, and the method of distance determination known as spectro-scopic parallax relies on this principle.

There are subleties in spectral classification which indicate whether a star really is a main-sequence object, but they are not easy to apply to faint cluster stars. Even simple spectra are time-consuming to obtain, and a measure of a star's colour is adopted instead to characterise properties. If we measure the brightness of a star at two wavelengths, in the blue (B) and visible (V), we can simultaneously determine its colour and magnitude. A plot of V against B-V is the colour-magnitude diagram, and the difference between the diagram we have explained here and those in Figures 4, 5 and 7 is that in the latter three cases the V magnitude has been converted into the absolute magnitude (M_v), which is the brightness an object would display at a distance of 10 pc.

If we made up a colour-magnitude diagram for a given cluster with V plotted against B-V and then made up a diagram for a second cluster at twice the distance the colours of the stars would not change, but their brightness would be reduced by about 1.5 mag. In a diagram for this second cluster, therefore, the entire main-sequence would be shifted 1.5 mag down the diagram, and we would immediately recognise that the second cluster was more distant than the first.

This is not the end of the story, however. We have determined distances only in a relative fashion - we can say only that cluster A is twice as distant as cluster B. To determine absolute distances we must measure the distance of one cluster by other means. The cluster chosen to calibrate all others is the Hyades. It has been known for some decades that Hyades stars move in the sky to a point of convergence in Gemini, this being an effect of parallax. The stars really follow parallel paths, but due to the parallax we can define the exact direction of motion in space of the Hyades relative to the Sun. Only under such circumstances can one relate the measured radial velocities and proper motions of the stars to determine their distance. Cluster distances can therefore be determined by fitting their main-sequence to that of the Hyades.

Appendix 3.

With regard to globular clusters, main-sequence fitting involves too many corrections to be as accurate as could be wished; also it requires observations which are far from easy to obtain. Bearing this in mind, it is advantageous that another method of distance determination is at hand, that of using RR Lyrae variable stars.

RR Lyrae variables are present in varying numbers in many globular clusters. They are to be found in the blue regions of the horizontal branches of numerable clusters, and objects such as Palomar 4, with only a red stub of a horizontal branch, contain no RR Lyrae stars. These stars have periods of less than one day, and are Population II objects. With the absolute magnitudes of RR Lyrae variables known, the distance moduli for these stars in clusters can be obtained and a distance figure derived. Certain corrections may be applied, as for the effects of interstellar absorption and certain intrinsic parameters, but no great problem is posed by any of these. This method of deriving the distance of globular clusters is the most reliable, and was used 50 years ago by Shapley and Sawyer.

Not all globular clusters contain RR Lyrae variables, however; metal-rich clusters with low z contain either none or, at best, only a few relative to the higher latitude metal-poor clusters. In such cases an aid in obtaining distances can be to use the absorption in front of such objects.

For open clusters the use of classical Cepheid variables, Population I objects with periods between one and fifty days, can be used to obtain distances, but the number of known Cepheids in open clusters is not great. Many clusters have none at all, while a very few clusters harbour more than one.

A further method for open clusters utilises a correlation between the Trumpler type of a cluster and its intrinsic diameter. In this procedure a nearby cluster of relatively well-determined distance and given type is compared with a more distant cluster of identical type. However, it is felt that this is not too reliable method. Error percentages are, nonetheless, inherent in all distance measures, 3-colour photometry of cluster stars, for example, giving rise to errors of the order of 20%. For this reason, considerable effort is expended in order to reduce such errors as much as possible.

APPENDIX 4.

PHOTOGRAPHIC SOURCES FOR
OPEN AND GLOBULAR CLUSTERS.

Below are listed a small number of sources in which photographs of many clusters of both types can be found. Most of these are reproduced in professional astronomical journals, which are available in astronomical libraries, such as that of the Royal Astronomical Society. The concentration is upon less well-known objects, as many popular books on astronomy reproduce pictures of the more common examples.

Open Clusters.

Markarian, B.E.	1952, A Photographic Atlas of Clusters and Nebulae. Moscow. (Includes the clusters NGC 366, 637, 663, 1502, 2362, 6405, 6475, 6494, 6823, 6871, 6913, 7160, 7510, 7788).
Grubussich, R.	1965, Zs. f. Ap., 60, 256. (Markarian 50).
Kirat, A.	1969, Astron. & Astrophys. 2, 22-27. (Ba 6, NGC 2254).
Racine, R.	1969, Astr. J. 74, 847. (Ros 4).
Pismis, P.	1970, Bull. Obs. Tonantzintla y Tacubaya, 5, 219-227. (NGC 2174-5).
Rahim, M.	1970, Astron. & Astrophys. 9, 221-226. (NGC 2236).
Yilmaz, F.	1970, Astron. & Astrophys. 8, 213-222. (NGC 7226, 7245, IC 1442, Be 94).
Van den Bergh, S. Heeringa, R.	1970 Astron. & Astrophys. 9, 209-215. (NGC 7142).
Wagner, R.	1971, Astron. & Astrophys. 14, 283-292. (Ba 89, Be 68).
Sanders, W.L.	1972, Astron. & Astrophys. 19, 155-158. (NGC 6819).
Wooden II, W.H.	1974, Astron. & Astrophys. 13, 218-225. (K 4, Ba 10).
Turner, D.G. Herbst, W.	1976, PASP 88, 308-311. (Lynds 810).
Lauberts, A.	1976, Astron. & Astrophys. 52, 3091311. (3 new distant clusters).

Appendix 4.

Globular Clusters.

Alcaino, G.   1971, Astron. & Astrophys. 13, 287-292.
                                (NGC 4833).

Rosino, L.   1972, in Variable Stars in Globular Cluster
Pinto, G.   and Related Systems. Ed. J.D. Fernie. Reid
T. Lloyd Evans,   (Palomar 2, NGC 104, 6388, 6553).
Menzies, J.W.

Alcaino, G.   1973, Atlas of Globular Clusters with Colou
                                Magnitude Diagrams. Universidad Catolica de
                                Chile.
                                (Numerous Clusters including two Palomar
                                 objects).

Hesser, J.C.   1976, PASP 88, 849-857.
                                (NGC 6304, 6352, 6441).

APPENDIX 5.
BIBLIOGRAPHY.

General.

Becvar, A.	1960, Atlas Coeli Katalog.	Prague.
Glyn Jones, K.	1968, Messier's Nebulae and Star Clusters.	Faber.
Alter, G. Balázs, B. Ruprecht, J.	1970, Catalogue of Star Clusters and Associations.	Budapest.
Bastos, A.	1974, Celestial Objects and Satellite Astronomy	Europ. Space Res. Org.

Open Clusters.

Becker, W.	1972, in The Role of Schmidt Telescopes in Astronomy. (Ed. U. Haug).	SRC/ESO.
Burki, G. Maeder, A.	1973, Astron. & Astrophys. 25, 71-77.	
Fawley, W.M.	1974, Ap. J. 193, 367-372.	
Fitzgerald, M.P. Moffat, A.F.J.	1974, Astr. J. 79, 873-884.	
Fitzgerald, M.P. Moffat, A.F.J.	1974, PASP 86, 480-485.	
Garrison, R.F. Kormendy, J.	1974, Journ. Roy. Astr. Soc. Canada, 68, 263.	
Sanduleak, N.	1974, PASP 86, 74-75.	
Strom, S.E. & K.M. Carrasco, L.	1974, PASP 86, 798-805.	
Grasdalen, G.L. Carrasco, L.	1975, Astron. & Astrophys. 43, 259-265.	
Hassan, S.M.	1975, Astron. & Astrophys. Supp. 20, 255-267.	
Samson, W.L.	1975, Astrophys. Sp. Sci. 34, 377-386.	
Wallenquist, A.	1975, Nova Acta Regiae Soc. Sci. Upsaliensis Ser. V:A 2, 1-98.	

Appendix 5.

Fitzgerald, M.P.   1976, Astron. & Astrophys, 50, 149-152.
Moffat, A.F.J.

McClure, R.D.   1977, Ap. J. 214, 111-123.
Twarog, B.A.

Moffat, A.F.J.   1977, Ap. J. 215, 106-118.
Fitzgerald, M.P.
Jackson, P.D.

Globular Clusters.

Arp, H.C.   1965, in Galactic Structure.   Chicago
         Stars & Stellar Systems, Vol. 5.
         (Ed. A. Blauuw & M. Schmidt).

Rosino, L.   1972, in Variable Stars in Globular Reidel
Pinto, G.   Clusters & Related Systems.
         (Ed. J.D. Fernie).

Alcaino, G.   1973, Atlas of Globular Clusters   Chile
         with Colour-Magnitude Diagrams.

Dickens, R.J.   1974, in Research Programmes for ESO/SRC/CERN
         the New Large Telescopes.
         (Ed. A. Reiz).

Harris, W.   1974, Journal Roy. Astr. Soc. Canada,
Racine, R.   68, 263.

Kukarkin, B.V.   1974, The Globular Star Clusters.   Moscow

Bahcall, N.A.   1976, Ap. J. Lett. 207, L181-184.
Hausman, M.A.

Gursky, H.   1976, Ap. J. 208, 47-51.
Bahcall, J.N.

Harris, W.E.   1976, PASP 88, 377-379.
Hesser, J.A.

Wehlau, A.   1977, Astr. J. 82, 137-149.
Hogg, H.S.

West, R.M.   1979, ESO Sci. Preprint No. 41.
Bartaya, R.A.